Rachael Ray's Open House Cookbook

Rachael Ray's Open House Cookbook

Over 200 Recipes for Easy Entertaining

LAKE ISLE PRESS
NEW YORK

All inquiries should be addressed to:

Lake Isle Press, Inc.
2095 Broadway, Suite 404
New York, NY 10023

lakeisle@earthlink.net

Distributed to the trade by National Book Network, Inc.
4720 Boston Way
Lanham, MD 20706
Phone: 1(800)462-6420
www.nbnbooks.com

Library of Congress Catalog Card Number: 99-73540

ISBN: 1-891105-04-3

Book design by Liz Trovato

Photography by Rick Siciliano

First printing, October 1999

To my family

Love, Rachael

Acknowledgments

Thanks, once again, to Hiroko Kiiffner and the wonderful designers and editors who make my chicken scratches look like a book.

Thanks to all the fans of *The 30-Minute Meal*. I love the notes and ideas—keep them coming!

Thanks to Dan DiNicola, still as good to know as he is to work with.

Thanks to WRGB and the gang at the Golub Corporation for all of their continued support.

A very special thank you to Rob and Donna Slack, owners of La Cabanna Lodge on Glen Lake, NY. All of our party pictures were taken on location at this spectacular Adirondack lodge.

Thank you to Villa Italia Pasticceria of Schenectady, NY for the incredible pastries provided for our parties. Yum!

Thanks to my family and friends for continuing to inspire this work.

Special thanks to my mom, Elsie Scuderi— without her, this book would not have been possible. Mom, thanks for sticking by me when I was too much of a pain for anyone else to stand. I love you.

Continued thanks to my dog, Boo, for eating the mistakes.

Contents

A Note About Ingredients

When it comes to recipes, I am more relaxed about measurements than other cooks. Ingredients are called for in both measured and freehand terms, e.g., 2 tablespoons extra-virgin olive oil or twice-around the pan. I use this technique to free the cook from the rigid nature of measures and gadgets. Cooking really is more an art than a science. As you become more creative in the kitchen, you will discover that you were born with the most important instruments, your hands and your palate. Learn to trust them.

Also, I do not specify a particular kind of butter for a reason. If you generally use unsalted butter because of dietary needs or personal preference, use it in these recipes. If you are more accustomed to salted butter, add your seasonings with a lighter hand. The choice is yours and depends on what you prefer.

Personally, I rarely use altered or reduced-fat products. However, your opinion is more important in your kitchen, so substitute freely to make the recipes more comfortable for you. If you prefer to use reduced-fat cheese and dairy products, just keep in mind that consistencies of dips, spreads or sauces will be slightly thinner. Always season to taste.

Introduction

It was a weeknight community awards dinner at a local Italian-American banquet house—white linens and stuffed chicken on the tables, in the background speeches thanking loved ones are heard over a crackling microphone. As dishes were cleared, the crowd rose in unison to make quick good-byes, intending to get out to their cars before the next guy. Then something extraordinary happened.

Music suddenly filled the air—familiar, happy, all-consuming music. (Who even realized there was a DJ? Nothing played earlier had made any impression on this group.) But now it was as if each person in the room were being whispered a delicious secret at precisely the same moment. Hats and coats were dropped, ladies hid their handbags under soiled napkins, and all present converged on the makeshift dance floor in the center of the banquet hall.

The events of the next several hours remain a vague, yet intense blurred memory. We were spinning around a dance floor, passing from one partner to the next—those who had until moments before been strangers—turning and twirling with smiling faces, everyone passing in front of one's eyes too swiftly to focus. This was a night that one would need a new word to describe, a night that was just beginning.

The music stopped as suddenly as it had started. A strange silence fell over the room. We remained quiet, a bit in shock, trying to reconstruct what had just taken place. Here's where the story might otherwise have ended, but then something wonderful happened again.

We began to exchange breathless sentences—he is a local hairdresser, she a mother of four, this man a new father, that man just retired. Someone boldly suggested that we not let the evening end—it was the hairdresser who lived nearby with his wife—and in response, we moved on.

Our caravan arrived at their house, filing in through the kitchen door. Instinctively knowing what to do, we made ourselves at home and pulled chairs up to the kitchen table. The table itself was a beautiful sight. It was long and wide and completely clean—no cloths or placemats, napkin holders or knickknacks—a blank canvas. It was old and loved, and worn, with a dozen chairs around it, enough to imagine a large family and many friends gathered around it. You could hear the echoes of laughter, passionate debates, and countless choruses of anniversary and birthday songs, to which we added our voices. The conversation grew animated.

The canvas of our table was quickly painted with plates of provolone and fontina, hunks of dried sausage and bread, jugs of homemade wine. We ate and drank and discussed all the things usually not discussed in groups—religion, politics, and family. We talked about everything else as well: movies, music, sports, travel, and the weather.

At two in the morning the patriarch made his appearance. At ninety-two, awakened from a sound sleep by a dozen noisy strangers, this man couldn't have been more pleased to join us. He was concerned about making a proper entrance, so he had shaved and dressed in his best shirt and trousers before coming downstairs.

The man was frail, but his presence strong. Standing at the end of the room, he spoke to us in Italian dialect. Strangely, we all understood what he was saying. He welcomed us, introduced himself, and humbly gestured that he wished to provide us with some entertainment. He pushed his sleeves up, slid his elastic watch band up his forearm and then picked up his concertina. As he began the familiar Italian melody "Whe-Marie," a Fellini-esque blond rose from her seat and sang, her throaty voice a sultry presence in the room. She crossed the floor and the old man came to meet her. He was suddenly in his prime again. Never missing a note, he raised the squeeze box over her head and played on with the beauty cradled in his arms.

Oh, what a night! This was better than any and every party I'd ever been to. We enjoyed the simple pleasures of this home, this truly open house, almost until dawn.

There was a time before video games, VCRs, and personal computers when people — friends, family, and neighbors — were their own entertainment. We did not plan and schedule every minute of every day. We had no use for home-entertaining divas and gurus because we did not care to formalize and accessorize our leisure time. Work was hard, and when it was over, this was our time to relax, visit with each other, and eat. Life was informal and we would drop in on one another. Somehow there was always enough food and drink to go around.

This book is a plea to return, if only for a moment, to this other time and place. I hope all who open this book use it to open their houses and their hearts.

—RACHAEL RAY

A News Update

The 30-Minute Meal is still one of the station's most popular features and I still cook while Rachael instructs. It's totally spontaneous, and the general theme remains, "If Dan can do it, so can you." I'm happy and proud to be part of the enterprise, and what makes me happiest is the fact that we attract viewers of all ages, that we are sharing something valuable, and that people once afraid to tackle a meal are now doing it.

The best, most rewarding compliment came from Robin, a working mother who made a pasta dish Rachael and I had prepared on the show. "My husband doesn't like pasta very much," she wrote, "but the night I made Rachael's dish, he had two helpings. He said to me, 'This is the best meal you've made in the ten years we've been married.' P.S. The kids loved it too."

With memories like these—thousands of letters and e-mail requests—I'm happy to add my own two cents to Rachael's wonderful observations about sharing, cooking, and, in the process, having a lot of fun.

—Dan DiNicola

Company's
Coming

Parties
You Can Prepare
and Attend

Perfect Party Tips

When it comes to parties, less is more.

When we attend a party, we are more interested in the people than the food. We want to talk and mingle and relax. We eat food in small amounts over the course of an entire afternoon or evening.

When we prepare a party, we forget all that. We get excited and a little nervous about what to have and how much of it to make. We try to offer a little of everything because we just can't decide on any one theme. The menu then turns into a lot of everything in the last seventy-two hours before the gathering, when we get worried that everyone will want the one thing we have the least of.

On the night of the party, we put all the food out, the moment everyone arrives. We spend the evening replating, replenishing, and doing the dishes. Then, suddenly, it's over. People are leaving before we've even had the chance to chat with them. We beg stragglers to take home weighty doggie bags of leftovers so food will not go to waste. Sound familiar?

Think about the following tips before your next gathering. They're based on what we all know as guests, but sometimes forget as hosts—the most important being, remember to RELAX!

1. Invite people you are comfortable with and those who will be comfortable with each other. This sounds ridiculously obvious, but it's advice we seldom follow. Save the networking for another time and place—don't bring politics, office or otherwise, into your home.

2. KISS—Keep It Super Simple. Pick a menu and stick to it. Produce a reasonable amount of food, following the guidelines and suggestions offered with the recipes.

3. Tailor your offerings to reflect your personality and preferences. You cannot be all things to all people. Please yourself first with your menu. You will find food much easier to handle and prepare if it appeals to your own taste buds.

4. Decorate your tables and platters with what you already have or what you can get for free. Be creative! Before planning your party, go on a scavenger hunt throughout your home.

From the garden shed, gather terracotta pots. When inverted, they make great risers for platters on a buffet. Small pots make terrific holders for flatware. Gather your potted plants and cut your flowers to mix in and among the spread of foods.

Look from room to room in your home in a whole new way. Big, heavy mirrors can be taken off the wall and turned into wonderful serving boards for antipasto or fruit and cheese. Mix and match the dishes you've packed away for years—you might find that they're just the thing for today.

Antipasto Party

Antipasto means "before the meal," but put out enough selections, and they make a meal. This easy gathering is best centered around the kitchen. **All of these recipes will feed 20 to 25 guests.**

Menu

Bruschetta and Crostini with Assorted Toppings

Olive, Meat, and Cheese Board with Giardiniera and Pepperoncini

Stuffed Dates

Fresh Figs and Gorgonzola with Hazelnuts

Italian Horns (Stuffed Sliced Genoa Salami)

Mamma's Roasted Red Peppers

Melon and Prosciutto

Crudités with Bagna Cauda (Garlic and Oil Dip)

Taralli (fennel and black pepper biscuits, available in Italian markets)

Wine biscuits (available in fancy food markets or wine shops)

Italian Cookies and Pastries with Fresh Fruit Tray

Coffee and Sambuca

Drinks

Italian slushes

San Pellegrino mineral water and lemon wedges

San Pellegrino sodas: bitter, lemon, orange

Italian wines: Chianti, Barolo, Pinot Grigio

Two days before your party:
Do the shopping.

One day before your party:
Cube and slice meats and cheeses and refrigerate in big Baggies. Make your roasted peppers. Chop vegetables for crudités and put on platters. Wrap bacon-stuffed dates. Wash your glasses and set up bar area. Set out disposables: party napkins, plates, and cocktail picks.

Day of your party:
Make your white bean topping. Stuff salami and dates and assemble fresh figs.

Two hours before guests arrive:
Make crostini. Wrap prosciutto and melon bites. Platter your meats and cheeses, olives, giardiniera, pepperoncini, and roasted peppers.

One hour before guests arrive:
Chop up tomato caponata. Arrange your platters and countertops.

Last-minute preparations:
Make bagna cauda as party begins. Cook bacon-wrapped stuffed dates.

Bruschetta and Crostini

Bruschetta, the Italian word for charred, is made by toasting bread under or over fire, then rubbing with cracked garlic and drizzling with olive oil. *Crostini* are Italian canapés, small toasts that may or may not contain garlic, traditionally with toppings. Serve any of the following spreads with 1 recipe of either bruschetta or crostini.

Bruschetta

makes 100 toasts

3 baguettes, sliced into rounds
6 large cloves garlic, cracked and
**   removed from skin**

Extra-virgin olive oil, for drizzling

Broil or grill bread rounds until crisp and toasted golden brown. Work in small batches to avoid burning toasts by having too many to handle. Rub toasts with garlic and drizzle with oil.

Crostini

Makes 100 toasts.

3 baguettes or other loaves of crusty
**   bread, sliced at bakery counter**
1 cup extra-virgin olive oil
2 cloves garlic, crushed
1/2 cup grated Parmigiano or

Romano cheese
6 sprigs fresh thyme, leaves pulled
**   from stems and chopped**
Black pepper, to taste

Heat oven to 325°F.

Spread sliced bread on cookie sheets in single layer. Toast in hot oven for 5 minutes and remove. Preheat broiler.

Heat oil and garlic in small pan over medium heat till garlic speaks by sizzling in the oil.

With a pastry brush, dot each toast with a bit of garlic oil. Grind a touch of pepper over toasts on trays. Sprinkle with a touch of cheese and chopped thyme, then, one tray at a time, lightly toast under broiler.

Collect crostinis in a basket or on a large platter and loosely cover with aluminum foil once completely cool.

Eggplant Spread: Poor Man's Caviar

1 large eggplant
3 cloves garlic, crushed
3 tablespoons extra-virgin olive oil
   (3 times around the pan)

A handful chopped fresh flat-leaf
   parsley
Coarse salt and black pepper, to taste
A pinch ground cumin

Heat oven to 425°F.

Prick skin of eggplant several times on one side only. Rest eggplant on rack one shelf from top of oven, pricked side up. Roast whole eggplant 20 to 25 minutes, or until eggplant begins to feel soft to a quick touch.

Remove eggplant from oven and let stand till cool enough to handle. Using a paring knife, peel black outer skin away like a banana. Work over a plate to catch the juices. Dump meat and juice into a food processor.

Heat garlic cloves in oil in a small saucepan over medium-low heat. Sauté garlic for a minute or so to infuse the oil with the garlic flavor. Dump oil and garlic into processor with eggplant. Add parsley, salt, pepper, and the pinch cumin. Pulse the blender and grind the mixture until it's smooth. Serve with crostini toasts.

Tomato and Onion Topping

12 plum tomatoes, seeded and diced
1 small white onion, minced
2 handfuls fresh flat-leaf parsley
    tops, chopped (about 1/2 cup)

Coarse salt and black pepper, to
    taste
3 tablespoons extra-virgin olive oil
    (3 times around the bowl)

Seed and chop tomatoes and let stand in a colander to drain for 15 minutes. To seed, split tomatoes lengthwise and squeeze gently over sink. Toss tomatoes with onion, parsley, salt, pepper, and a drizzle of olive oil. Serve at room temperature with garlic toasts.

VARIATION:

20 leaves of fresh basil, thinly sliced, may be substituted for the parsley.

White Bean and Rosemary Spread

2 cans (15 1/2 ounce) cannellini beans,
    drained and rinsed
2 cloves garlic, crushed
3 tablespoons extra-virgin olive oil
    (3 times around the pan)

4 sprigs fresh rosemary, leaves
    stripped from stems
Coarse salt and black pepper, to
    taste

Place beans in food processor. Heat garlic and oil in a small pan over medium-low heat and sauté for 2 or 3 minutes. Dump garlic and oil in processor with rosemary, salt, and pepper. Pulse processor until smooth paste forms. Serve with garlic toasts or with garlic and herb Terra chips.

Olive, Meat, and Cheese Board with Giardiniera and Pepperoncini

1/2 pound each, hot and sweet, sliced sopressata (from your deli counter or Italian market)

1/2 pound Abruzzese or Calabrese sausage (available in deli area)

1 pound prosciutto cotto (Citterio brand is widely available), rubbed with rosemary

2 1/2 pounds mixed Italian cheeses (from your choice of fontina, fontina Val Dosta, taleggio, Asiago, sharp provolone, pepato, Parmigiano Reggiano, smoked mozzarella)

1 quart mixed olives in herbs: green Sicilian, Kalamata, oil cured, Picholine, Niçoise. (Mixed olives are available in bulk bins near the deli and cheese cases in your market.)

1 quart giardiniera, drained (see Note)

1 jar (16 ounces) pepperoncini

Sweet, pickled cherry peppers, to garnish

1 recipe Italian Horns (see page 24)

Slice sausages and refrigerate in Baggies till you are ready to serve. Cube or shave a few pieces of each cheese and refrigerate in Baggies. When party time nears, place small dishes of olives around a big cutting board. Place fans and piles of meats and cheeses on the board. Decorate with drained giardiniera, pepperoncini, sweet pickled cherry peppers, and Italian Horns.

Note: Giardiniera is Italian hot, pickled vegetable relish found on the Italian foods or condiment aisles.

Stuffed Dates

30 pitted dates   15 slices thin, center-cut bacon
30 Diamond brand smokehouse   Chopped parsley, to garnish
   almonds

Stuff each date with an almond. Cut bacon strips in half. Roll half a slice of bacon around each date. Chill until ready to serve.

To serve, place date and bacon rolls on a broiler pan. Preheat oven to 400°F. Cook dates 12 minutes, until bacon is golden. Remove from slotted broiler pan to serving dish and garnish with a little chopped parsley.

Figs and Gorgonzola with Hazelnuts

$1/2$ cup chopped hazelnuts   Juice of $1/2$ lemon
$1/3$ pound Gorgonzola cheese   2 tablespoons balsamic vinegar
15 fresh figs, halved   Salt and pepper, to taste
4 tablespoons extra-virgin olive oil
   (a couple of glugs)

Place nuts in a metal pie or cake pan and toast at 350°F for 10 minutes. Remove and cool. With a teaspoon, place a few creamy crumbles of Gorgonzola on each half fig and arrange on a platter. Mix oil, lemon juice, balsamic vinegar, salt, and pepper. Sprinkle figs with toasted nuts and a drizzle of dressing. Serve slightly chilled or at room temperature.

Italian Horns

1/2 pound sliced Genoa salami
1 small jar olive tapenade (available in Italian markets and in Italian food aisles)

1/2 pound ricotta salata cheese, crumbled
1/4 cup drained, finely chopped hot or sweet peppers

Make a cut halfway across each slice of salami. Spread salami slice with a touch of tapenade and roll it into a cone shape, overlapping one "tab" behind the other. Fill "horns" with a little crumbled cheese and top with chopped hot or sweet peppers.

Mamma's Roasted Red Peppers

6 red bell peppers, halved and seeded

1 large paper sack

A drizzle extra-virgin olive oil
2 cloves crushed garlic, minced
A handful chopped fresh flat-leaf parsley and a little coarse salt

Preheat broiler. Place peppers skin side up on a cookie sheet. Place sheet with peppers under broiler till skins are charred all over. Leave the door a bit ajar as peppers cook so steam does not take the first two layers of skin off your nose when you open the oven door. Dump peppers into a big paper sack and roll it up tightly. Let stand 10 minutes. Remove peppers and peel away skin over sink. Place peeled peppers on a board and cut into strips. Place strips on a dish and chill until ready to serve. Thirty minutes before serving, let peppers come to room temperature. Drizzle with oil and a sprinkle of minced garlic mixed with parsley and salt.

Melon and Prosciutto

1 cantaloupe, peeled and seeded   **¹/₃ pound (20 to 25 slices) very
thinly sliced prosciutto di Parma**

Slice each melon in half, then each half into ten thin slices. Cut each slice into thirds, or smaller slices in half, to yield about 50 pieces. Cut sliced prosciutto in half. Wrap each piece of melon with a half slice of prosciutto. Platter and chill. Serve or pass with a small glass or dish of colored or frilled toothpicks.

Crudités with Bagna Cauda

I have the coolest dish to serve this in. I found it at Sur La Table, a kitchen store. Along with my purchase, I received a pretty authentic recipe for this traditional Italian dip for veggies that is so much tastier than anything ever created with sour cream. These serving bowls, shallow pots with a little hole in the base for placing a candle, are really hard to find. Use a fondue pot or preheated Pyrex bowl to serve. It's worth improvising to enjoy this yummy coating even if the container is a little awkward. No one will care what the serving dish looks like once they taste the dip.

For dipping up to 100 blanched and chilled vegetable sticks. To blanch, immerse vegetable sticks for 15 to 20 seconds in simmering water, rinse in cold water, and drain. Try red bell pepper strips, green beans, zucchini sticks, celery, baby carrots, cherry tomatoes, and artichoke hearts (packed in water, and drained).

**Mixed vegetable sticks, blanched
    and chilled**

1 cup extra-virgin olive oil
3 tablespoons butter
6 cloves garlic, minced
**2 cans flat anchovies, drained and
    chopped**

2 pinches crushed red pepper flakes
**A handful chopped fresh flat-leaf
    parsley**
**2 tablespoons capers, smashed with
    flat of knife**
Coarse black pepper, to taste

Heat oil, butter, and garlic over medium heat. When garlic begins to speak by sizzling in oil, add anchovies and crushed red pepper flakes and reduce heat to low. Stir until anchovies melt into oil. Add parsley, capers, and pepper. Serve warm.

Drinks

Place bottles of chilled San Pellegrino mineral water around the kitchen and a small stack of glasses or party cups alongside. The green bottles will decorate your spread.

Ask for tips from your wine shopkeeper on reasonably priced Italian wines, or check out BestCellars.Net on your computer for some terrific wine tips and selections, all under ten bucks.

To offer Italian slushes, fill a wineglass with scoops of Italian lemon ice or sorbet and pour dry red wine over it.

Cookies and Other Dolce

I do not bake. My advice is to never attempt a party that you both cook and bake for—two different disciplines. Cooking is loose, a little of this and a little of that. Once you get into the swing, you can have your hands in five different things and still know what you're doing. Baking is more of a science. You must measure and be precise. Trust me—order the cookies from a nice Italian bakery. Just don't forget the pignoli cookies and the sfogliatelle.

If pastry and cookies seem too heavy, especially in summer, serve fruit and a selection of Italian ices.

Tapas Party

Tapas are the "little dishes" of Spain. These pretty and very easy to make foods are wonderful party offerings. Since they are quite substantial, you don't need to make many varieties. Tapas should be served warm. Center this party around the kitchen and chat through the last-minute preparations, sharing the dishes with your friends from beginning to end. Pace the offerings. Cook a few tapas and let everyone enjoy them, yourself included. Then prepare a few more. This is the way they are eaten in Spain—over the course of a few hours with lots of conversation and a little wine. **The recipes for this party will feed 20.**

Menu

Tortillas (Egg Pies)

Herbed Chicken Tapas

Sherry-Beef Tapas

Chorizo Tapas

Tomato Bread

Seared Scallops

Mushroom Caps in Garlic Sauce

Mixed herbed Olives and Cornichons

Spanish cheeses (mahon, manchego,

Cabrales blue—whatever you can find,

up to a total of 1½ pounds.)

Grapes, Pears, and Fresh Figs, in season,

a total of 2 to 2½ pounds (a little fruit goes a long way)

Rioja sangria, Italian wines, sparkling water

Almond cookies and citrus sorbets

One day before your party:

Do your shopping. Trim meats and place on paper-towel lined dishes. Cover and refrigerate. Set out glasses and disposables.

Day of your party:

Assemble all of your serving dishes near the stove so you can keep filling them. Place shot glasses filled with long bamboo picks or skewers around counters or serving table with small piles of party napkins alongside. Trim breads for Chorizo Tapas (see recipe page 32).

One to two hours before guests arrive:

Make tortillas and cover loosely with plastic wrap. Cut meat into pieces. Have all ingredients near the stove to assemble first tapas offerings.

More Party Tips

• If you are throwing a party for a family member, decorate with the things he or she loves—books or sheet music, art supplies or sports equipment. Anything can be turned into a decoration if you set your mind to it.

• Greenery is as close as your own backyard. Trim a few branches, collect a few pine cones—no one sets a more elegant table than Mother Nature.

• The only things you should have left to purchase when you have gone through your house are candles and napkins. Try the dollar store for these—really. There are candles in every shape and size and wonderful prints or solid-colored disposables in every so-called dollar or "junk store." Go and see for yourself—it's usually a fun, inexpensive shopping spree.

Tortillas (Egg Pies)

You need a 7- or 8-inch nonstick skillet and a flat dinner plate to make these egg pies.

Potato Tortilla

**4 tablespoons extra-virgin olive oil
(4 times around the pan)
2 medium white potatoes, peeled
and very thinly sliced, seasoned
with a little salt**

**Half a large sweet onion, thinly sliced
4 large eggs
Coarse salt, to taste
A splash cold water (2 teaspoons)**

Heat oil in your skillet over medium heat. Place salted potato and the onion in pan in alternating single layers and gently cook, turning occasionally, not allowing potatoes to brown, for 10 minutes, or until potatoes are tender. Beat the eggs till frothy with a pinch of salt and a splash of cold water. Pour over potatoes. Use a spatula to lift potatoes and onions so liquids can settle under them. Shake pan to keep omelet from sticking as the eggs begin to set. Continue to shake pan and cook until tortilla is set. Place a plate over top of pan, flip, and transfer inverted tortilla to plate. Return eggs to pan on flip side. Shake pan to keep tortilla from sticking. Let the bottom set, then flip another time or two, mostly because it makes you feel incredibly talented. Place tortilla on serving plate and let cool before covering loosely with plastic wrap until ready to serve, at room temperature. Wipe pan and return to stove for next tortilla. To serve, cut into 10 small wedges. 3 tortillas will yield 30 small wedges.

Fontina and Mushroom Tortilla

16 small white mushroom caps,
cleaned and chopped
1 tablespoon extra-virgin olive oil
(once around the pan)
A pat (1 tablespoon) butter
A little fresh flat-leaf parsley,
chopped (a tablespoon or so)
Salt and pepper, to taste

Two tablespoons extra-virgin olive
oil (twice around the pan)
1 teaspoon truffle oil (optional)
6 large eggs and a splash heavy
cream or half-and-half
(2 teaspoons)
1/4 pound fontina cheese, thinly
sliced or shredded
Zest of 1 lemon
A little chopped fresh parsley, for
garnish

Sauté mushrooms in oil and butter over medium heat until tender. Sprinkle with parsley, salt, and pepper. Transfer to a paper towel-lined plate to cool.

Preheat broiler.

Wash out pan, dry, and return to medium heat. When pan is hot, add olive and truffle oils. Beat eggs with a splash of heavy cream or half-and-half. Fold mushrooms into eggs and pour into pan. Cook eggs, lifting bottom up with spatula to allow liquids to settle, until tortilla is set. Shake pan to keep tortilla from sticking. Cover pan with plate, turn and invert tortilla, then slide back into pan. Set the flip side, shaking pan to keep the tortilla from sticking, and flip a couple more times with the plate. You are too cool. Top evenly browned tortilla with fontina and place under broiler to melt and brown cheese. Transfer to serving plate and sprinkle with lemon zest and parsley. Allow tortilla to cool completely before covering loosely with plastic wrap until ready to serve, at room temperature. Cut pie into 10 wedges to serve.

Chorizo and Vegetable Confetti Tortilla

1/4 to 1/3 pound chorizo, chourico,
  or linguica, skinned and diced
1 small onion, diced
1 teaspoon extra-virgin olive oil
  (a drizzle)
1/4 green bell pepper, diced
1/4 red bell pepper, diced

3 tablespoons extra-virgin olive oil
  (3 times around the pan)
6 eggs, beaten
A handful frozen green peas,
  defrosted and drained
Pinch salt

Cook chorizo and onion in the teaspoon of olive oil over medium heat for 5 minutes. Add peppers and cook another minute or two. Transfer mixture to a plate. Rinse out pan and dry and return to medium heat. Add 3 tablespoons oil and heat while beating eggs. Fold a handful of peas and a pinch of salt into eggs. Add eggs to pan and set chorizo mixture on them. As eggs set, lift with spatula and allow liquids to continue to settle. When tortilla is set firmly, turn tortilla onto a plate and invert. Slide tortilla back into pan and cook till opposite side is set. Turn a few more times, then transfer to serving plate. Let cool until room temperature. Cover loosely with plastic wrap till ready to serve. Cut into 10 wedges.

Herbed Chicken Tapas

2 pounds chicken tenders
1/2 cup extra-virgin olive oil (3 glugs)
Juice of 1 lemon
2 stems fresh rosemary, leaves
  striped from stem and minced
  (1 tablespoon)

4 sprigs fresh thyme, leaves stripped
  and chopped
Coarse salt and fresh pepper, to
  taste

Toss chicken in oil, lemon juice, herbs, and salt and pepper. Get a nonstick pan smoking hot over medium-high heat. Add chicken tenders, half a batch at a time, lifting them out of marinade and shaking off excess before you add them. Cook 6 to 7 minutes, shaking pan frequently. Transfer to plate and repeat with next batch. After last batch, add any leftover marinade to pan and deglaze. Pour these juices over chicken. Serve with long picks and eat hot.

Note: Chicken "tenders" are chicken breast tenderloins, packaged and sold as such in supermarkets.

Sherry-Beef Tapas

2 pounds sirloin or tenderloin,
    trimmed and cut into 1-inch cubes
4 tablespoons extra-virgin olive oil
    (total)
8 cloves garlic, crushed

$2/3$ cup good sherry
Montreal Steak Seasoning (by
    McCormick) or coarse salt and
    black pepper, to taste

Let meat stand at room temperature for 30 minutes. Heat half of the oil in a big, nonstick skillet over medium-high heat till pan smokes. Add 4 cloves of the garlic and half the meat. Cook 3 minutes on each side. Remove meat bites to serving dish. Deglaze the pan with a big splash of half the sherry. Scrape up all the good bits and pour the juice over the meat. Sprinkle cooked meat bites with seasoning. Wipe out pan. Return pan to heat and repeat process with rest of meat.

Chorizo Tapas

A drop of extra-virgin olive oil
$3/4$ pound chorizo, skinned and
    sliced into thirty $1/2$-inch-thick
    slices cut on an angle
A splash dry red Spanish wine,
    such as Rioja

1 crusty baguette, sliced at bakery,
    trimmed of crusts and in thin
    $1 1/2$-inch squares

Toothpicks

Heat a drop of oil in a nonstick skillet over medium-high heat until pan smokes. Add chorizo slices and brown a minute or two on each side. Deglaze pan with a splash of wine and shake pan until wine evaporates. Scrape up all the good bits onto the chorizo. Remove from heat and stab a piece of bread, then a slice of chorizo, and transfer to a serving plate. Makes 30 pieces.

Tomato Bread

2 loaves crusty bread, sliced $^1/_2$ to $^3/_4$
    inch thick (about 35 to 40 slices)
2 ripe tomatoes

Extra-virgin olive oil for drizzling
Coarse salt, to taste

Toast bread under broiler in a single layer on cookie sheets until lightly golden.
Flip and toast opposite side. Rub half of a very ripe tomato into one side of 8 to
10 slices of bread. Repeat until all of the bread is coated with tomato juice. Drizzle
olive oil over tomato-juiced side of slices. Sprinkle with a pinch of coarse salt.

Seared Scallops

$2^1/_2$ pounds sea scallops (about
    40 scallops)

Extra-virgin olive oil
Coarse salt, to taste

Drain scallops and pat dry. Heat a drizzle of olive oil in a large nonstick skillet over
medium-high heat until pan is very hot. Place half the scallops in the pan at a time
in a single layer and cook for 2 minutes on each side, until golden in color. If scallops approach dark brown at any point, reduce heat a touch. Sprinkle caramelized
scallops with a pinch of coarse salt. Serve warm.

Mushroom Caps in Garlic Sauce

40 small whole mushroom caps
2 tablespoons extra-virgin olive oil
   (twice around pan)
2 tablespoons butter
12 cloves garlic, minced

$1/2$ cup Spanish sherry (a couple
   good splashes)
Coarse salt and black pepper, to taste
A handful fresh flat-leaf parsley,
   chopped

Brown mushrooms in olive oil and butter over medium-high heat. Add garlic and shake pan, cooking another minute. Douse pan with sherry. Reduce sherry by half, cooking another minute or two, shaking pan frequently. Sprinkle with salt, pepper, and a handful of parsley. Turn off heat and let stand till ready to serve.

Rioja Sangria

For every 10 guests.

1 large navel orange, half left whole,
   half thinly sliced, slices reserved
$1/4$ cup sugar (a handful)
2 cups orange juice, not from
   concentrate, no pulp

1 bottle (750 ml.) Spanish Rioja wine
$1/2$ cup Grand Marnier or Triple Sec

Ice, for glasses
A big pitcher

Using a veggie peeler, peel the outer skin off the whole half orange. In a small bowl, using the back of a spoon or a mortar and pestle, mush the orange skin with the sugar. Dump mushed peels into pitcher. Stir in juice. Add wine and liqueur and stir again. Cover and chill. Remove orange peels when ready to serve. Pour over ice and garnish with reserved orange slices. Olé, baby!

Pizza Party

There is no topping the pizza party. It goes with everything—opera to funk, sports to Oscars. For the perfect relaxed gathering, load up on toppings and just keep the pies coming throughout the evening. Cut them in wedges or small squares and stock up on napkins and beverages. If you are pressed for time, use storebought dough. If you do not have a pizza stone, make any of these pies on thin-crust Boboli pizza shells, available in any market. Mamma mia, this is a party!

For a party of 20

Menu

Pizza Margherita (basil, tomato and mozzarella)

The Smokin' Joe Robinson (onion, pancetta, smoked mozzarella)

Ode to the Beatles: The White Pizza (mozzarella, Parmigiano, and basil)

The Simon and Garfunkel (parsley, sage, rosemary, thyme)

Potato Pie (potato, onion, and fennel seed)

Wild Mushroom Pie (portobellos, criminis, shiitakes, thyme, fontina, chives)

Roman Street Pie (shredded zucchini, garlic, and Parmigiano)

The Sicilian (tomato, olive, tuna, and bread crumbs)

The Fisherman's Net (shrimp and clams)

The New Yorker (pizza sauce and 4 cheeses)

The Uptown New Yorker (tomato, anchovy, and capers)

The Downtown New Yorker (pizza sauce, sausage, pepperoni, prosciutto—a.k.a., The Salt-and-Fat, Can't-Beat-That Pie)

Green salad with balsamic vinaigrette

Olives and bread sticks

Fresh fruit for dessert (figs, grapes, pears, or berries drizzled with liqueur)

Italian ices

Beer, Italian sodas, mineral water, and wines

Serving Suggestions:
Mix and match eight pies, total—two each of four types makes life easier. Have four ready when guests arrive; make batches of two throughout the evening. Everyone will want to pitch in.

Day before your party:
Do your shopping. Set up bar and disposables.

Day of your party:
Make dough, if using homemade. Prepare as many toppings as you can.

An hour and a half before your party:
If using storebought raw dough, bring out to rest at room temperature and punch down.

Half an hour before guests arrive:
Place the first pie in the oven. While one cooks, ready the next. Pile 4 up for the first wave of guests. Wait till mid-party to cook the next batch.

Dough-Easy

Each dough recipe will make 2 pies, each yielding 12 thin wedges or 16, 2 by 2-inch squares.

1/4 cup lukewarm water
1 package active dry yeast
A couple pinches sugar (about 3/4 to 1 teaspoon)
2 1/2 cups all-purpose unbleached flour, plus a couple handfuls for kneading

A couple pinches coarse salt (about 3/4 to 1 teaspoon)
1/4 cup extra-virgin olive oil (3 times around the bowl), plus a drizzle to oil a large mixing bowl

In a big bowl, combine the 1/4 cup water with the yeast and sugar. Set the bowl aside and let the mixture hang out for 10 minutes, until it's all foamy and bubbly.

Mix 1 cup of the flour with a couple of pinches of salt in a big bowl. Add the yeast mixture and stir with a big wooden spoon. Add the olive oil to the bowl, drizzling the oil 3 times around the bowl in a light stream. Add another cup of the flour to the bowl and keep stirring. When dough begins to form, remove the spoon and knead the dough. When you are kneading the dough, you can feel whether or not you *need* all of your flour. If it is raining outside, your flour might have already sucked up some moisture right out of the air, so you might need only 2 1/4 cups. Stop kneading the dough when it is smooth and stretchy and no longer sticky.

Pour a little oil into a second big bowl and spread it around the sides of the bowl with a pastry brush. Dump the dough into the oiled bowl and turn it around until it is smooth and a little glossy and evenly coated with oil. Cover dough with a damp kitchen towel.

Turn the oven on to 200°F for 5 minutes, then turn it off and place the covered bowl on the center rack on a pot holder pillow. (I don't know why the "pillow"; older Italians just do it that way and refuse to explain why.) Close the oven and let the dough rise till double in size, about 1 hour.

Cut dough in half and roll into balls. Chill until 45 minutes before you're ready to use.

Bring dough out and let rest in warm place for 45 minutes. Punch it down before stretching and rolling to make pie on floured or cornmeal-dusted peel or cookie sheet.

As soon as the dough comes out of fridge, preheat a pizza stone on the bottom rack of an oven set at 500°F for 45 minutes. Reduce heat to recommended baking temperature for each topping when pizza slides off peel and hits stone.

Pizza-Making Tips:

Spread your toppings on in very thin layers—serving soggy pie is all wet.

Always preheat a pizza stone for 45 minutes at 500°F on bottom rack of oven. Cook homemade pies at suggested temperature and lengths of time listed in recipes, usually until crispy and cheese or bread crumbs turn golden. If you are using storebought, precooked shells, preheat oven 10 minutes and cook on cookie sheet or perforated pizza pan for 10 to 12 minutes.

Build pizzas on a floured or cornmeal-dusted pizza peel (large wooden spatula) or cookie sheet, then transfer to pizza stone.

Topped Pies

Each recipe will make one pie. Cooking times are for raw dough, storebought or homemade. You can use toppings on prepared crusts, like thin-crust Boboli, but remember, they will cook in about half the time.

Pizza Margherita

1/2 recipe Dough-Easy or store-bought pizza dough

1/4 pound fresh mozzarella, thinly sliced

4 whole, canned plum tomatoes, drained, seeded, and chopped

6 fresh basil leaves, piled on top of one another, rolled into log, and slivered

A drizzle extra-virgin olive oil

A pinch coarse salt

To assemble, scatter mozzarella, plum tomatoes, and basil on dough and drizzle pie with olive oil and a pinch of salt.

Bake at 500°F for 12 to 15 minutes, or until crisp and brown.

The Smokin' Joe Robinson

1/2 recipe Dough-Easy or store-bought pizza dough

2 slices pancetta or bacon, diced

1 small onion, chopped

1/4 pound smoked fresh mozzarella, thinly sliced

Cracked black pepper, to taste

Drizzle extra-virgin olive oil

Cook pancetta in a small pan until fat is rendered. Remove from pan and drain on paper towels. Return pan to medium heat and cook onion until golden brown and soft. Spread thin layer of mozzarella on dough. Sprinkle bacon and onion on mozzarella. Drizzle with oil and cracked black pepper. Cook 12 to 15 minutes at 500°F.

Ode to the Beatles: The White Pizza

¹/₂ recipe Dough-Easy or store-
bought pizza dough

¹/₄ pound fresh mozzarella, thinly
sliced

A handful grated Parmigiano cheese
6 leaves fresh basil, piled up, rolled
into log, and thinly sliced
Drizzle extra-virgin olive oil

Top pizza dough with ingredients in order listed and cook 10 to 15 minutes at 500°F, or until crispy and golden.

The Simon and Garfunkel: Parsley, Sage, Rosemary, and Thyme Pie

¹/₂ recipe Dough-Easy or store-
bought pizza dough

A palmful fresh flat-leaf parsley,
chopped (2 tablespoons)
4 leaves fresh sage, piled one atop
the other, thinly sliced (about 1
tablespoon)
2 sprigs fresh rosemary, leaves
stripped and finely chopped

(about 1 tablespoon)
4 sprigs fresh thyme, leaves stripped
from stems, chopped (about 1
tablespoon)
¹/₄ cup ricotta salata or goat cheese
crumbles
2 ounces shredded fontina (a handful)
Drizzle extra-virgin olive oil
Black pepper, to taste

For a cheap pizza stone alternative, line bottom rack of oven with quarry tiles from a home improvement center.

For a super pizza supper, make 1 of any pie for every 2 people.

Cover dough with herbs. Crumble ricotta salata or goat cheese over herbs. Sprinkle with a little fontina, a drizzle of oil, and a few grinds of black pepper. Cook 12 to 15 minutes at 450°F until fontina turns golden and ricotta salata crumbles are brown at edges.

Potato Pie

¹/₂ recipe Dough-Easy or store-
    bought pizza dough

¹/₄ cup extra-virgin olive oil
2 small red- or white-skinned
    potatoes, very thinly sliced
1 small onion, thinly sliced

¹/₄ teaspoon fennel seed (a couple
    pinches)
A sprinkle coarse salt
A handful grated Parmigiano or
    Romano cheese
Chopped fresh parsley, for garnish

Heat olive oil over medium heat in small skillet. Add potatoes, onion, and fennel seed and cook gently, flipping occasionally, until tender. Remove to paper towel-lined plate. Spread on pizza dough in a thin layer and sprinkle with a pinch of salt and Parmigiano or Romano cheese. Cook 15 to 18 minutes at 450°F, or until edges of potatoes and onions begin to brown and crust is crisp. Remove from pizza stone and sprinkle with parsley.

Wild Mushroom Pie

¹/₂ recipe Dough-Easy or store
    bought pizza dough

2 tablespoons extra-virgin olive oil
    (twice around the pan)
1 small portobello mushroom cap,
    halved and thinly sliced
4 crimini mushroom caps, thinly
    sliced

2 shiitake mushroom caps, sliced
2 sprigs fresh rosemary, leaves
    stripped and finely chopped
¹/₄ pound fontina cheese, shredded
A drizzle extra-virgin olive oil
Salt and pepper, to taste
Chopped fresh parsley, to garnish

Heat olive oil in a small skillet and cook mushrooms and rosemary until dark and tender. Transfer to paper towel-lined plate to drain. Top pie with mushrooms and sprinkle with fontina. Drizzle with oil and sprinkle with salt and pepper. Cook 15 to 18 minutes, or until golden and crust is crispy. Top with chopped parsley.

Roman Street Pie

When Mamma and I were in Rome, this pie, along with cold water, was our pick-me-up every afternoon. Good fuel to on—enjoy.

1/2 recipe Dough-Easy or store-bought pizza dough

2 cloves garlic, minced
2 tablespoons extra-virgin olive oil

1 small zucchini, shredded with hand grater
Pinch coarse salt
A handful grated Parmigiano or Romano cheese

Cook garlic in olive oil over medium heat until garlic speaks by sizzling in oil. Add zucchini and cook gently until tender, 3 to 5 minutes. Transfer to paper towel-lined plate to drain. Sprinkle with salt. Spread the zucchini to edges of the dough. Top with grated cheese and a drizzle of oil. Cook 15 to 18 minutes at 450°F, or until crisp.

The Sicilian

1/2 recipe Dough-Easy or store-bought pizza dough

1 can (4 ounces) tuna in oil, Italian if you can find it, drained
12 oil-cured black olives, pitted and coarsely chopped
4 peeled canned plum tomatoes, drained, seeded, and diced

1 tablespoon capers, smashed with side of knife
A handful Italian bread crumbs (1/4 cup or so)
A drizzle extra-virgin olive oil
A pinch crushed red pepper flakes
Chopped fresh parsley, to garnish

Flake tuna across pie dough. Sprinkle with olives, tomatoes, capers, and bread crumbs. Drizzle pie with olive oil and add a pinch of crushed red pepper. Cook at 400°F for 12 to 15 minutes, or until crisp and bread crumbs are dark golden. Top pie with a sprinkle of parsley.

The Fisherman's Net

1/2 recipe Dough-Easy or store-bought pizza dough

16 small shrimp, peeled and deveined, tails removed, patted dry on paper towel
1 can (6 1/2 ounces) whole baby clams, drained very well
2 tablespoons extra-virgin olive oil

2 cloves garlic, minced
Salt and pepper, to taste
A pinch crushed red pepper flakes
A handful Italian bread crumbs
2 slices bacon or pancetta, chopped, browned, and drained (optional)
Chopped fresh parsley, for garnish
A wedge fresh lemon, to serve

Toss cleaned and dried shrimp and well-drained clams with oil, garlic, salt, pepper, and crushed red pepper flakes. Spread mixture evenly across pie dough. Sprinkle pie with a handful of bread crumbs, and the bacon bits, if you opt for that. Cook 10 to 12 minutes at 450°F, or until crisp and bread crumbs are golden. Remove pie from oven and sprinkle with parsley and a squeeze of 1 wedge of lemon.

The New Yorker

PIZZA SAUCE:
1 clove garlic, minced
1 tablespoon extra-virgin olive oil
1/2 small onion, minced
1/2 cup crushed tomatoes
1 tablespoon tomato paste
Pinch salt
Pinch sugar
1 sprig fresh oregano, chopped
   (1/2 teaspoon)

1/2 recipe Dough-Easy or store-bought pizza dough

1/4 pound total grated provolone, mozzarella, and Asiago cheeses (a couple handfuls of this blend per pie)
A sprinkle Parmigiano cheese

Heat garlic and oil in small pan. Add onion and cook over medium heat until soft and sweet. Add crushed tomatoes, tomato paste, salt, sugar, and oregano. Simmer 5 minutes and remove from heat. Spread sauce around pie, out to edges. Top with a layer of the blended Italian cheeses and a sprinkle of Parmigiano. Cook 15 minutes at 500°F, or until golden and crisp.

The Uptown New Yorker

1/2 recipe Dough-Easy or store-
  bought pizza dough

1 tablespoon extra-virgin olive oil
2 anchovy fillets
2 cloves garlic, minced
A pinch crushed red pepper flakes
4 canned whole plum tomatoes,
  drained, seeded, and diced

1 tablespoon capers, smashed with
  flat of knife
A handful black oil-cured olives,
  pitted and coarsely chopped
1/4 pound provolone cheese,
  shredded
Drizzle extra-virgin olive oil
A palmful chopped fresh flat-leaf
  parsley, for garnish

Heat oil, anchovies, garlic, and crushed red pepper flakes in a small pan over medium heat until anchovies melt into oil. Remove from heat and toss tomatoes in mixture. Spread tomato mixture over the pie in a very thin layer. Sprinkle with capers, olives, and provolone cheese. Drizzle pie with oil and cook 15 minutes at 450°F or until crisp and cheese is golden. Remove and sprinkle with parsley for garnish.

The Downtown New Yorker

1/2 recipe Dough-Easy or store-
  bought pizza dough

1 recipe Pizza Sauce (see page 43)
1/4 pound total grated provolone,
  mozzarella, and Asiago cheeses
  (a couple of handfuls of this blend
  per pie)

1/4 pound bulk sweet Italian
  sausage, browned and drained
4 slices slicing pepperoni from deli
  counter, chopped
2 slices prosciutto di Parma, chopped
A sprinkle Parmigiano cheese

Spread sauce across pie from the center out to edges. Sprinkle pie with cheeses and meats, saving Parmigiano for top. Cook 20 minutes at 450°F or until cheese is bubbling and golden.

Mix 'n Match Shindigs

Dips, Spreads, Pick-Ups, and Room-Temperature Entrées

Mix and match any two dips, any two spreads, any three pick-ups and any two entrées for a great party for up to twenty guests. Dips and spreads are done ahead. Pick-ups have their own do-ahead timing notes. Room temperature entrées should be finished in the last hour prior to the party, leaving you just enough time to slap on a fresh coat of lipstick or shave before the crowd gathers. And for once, you can enjoy your own party.

Dips

Groovy Green Goddess Dip

Makes 1 1/2 cups.

1 clove garlic, coarsely chopped
A handful fresh flat-leaf parsley
   (about 1/4 cup)
2 sprigs fresh tarragon
2 green onions, coarsely chopped
1 bunch watercress, stems removed,
   washed and dried (about 1/3 cup)
1 squirt anchovy paste (about 1 teaspoon) or 3 anchovies, minced
   and heated in microwave for 20
   seconds to melt

Juice of 1/2 lemon
Salt and pepper, to taste
1/2 cup mayonnaise or reduced-fat
   mayonnaise (a couple scoops)
1/2 cup sour cream or reduced-fat
   sour cream (a couple scoops)

In a food processor, grind all ingredients except mayonnaise and sour cream. Scrape into small mixing bowl and combine with mayonnaise and sour cream. Transfer to serving bowl and chill until ready to serve. This is yummy with hearts of romaine or spears of endive, cherry tomatoes, blanched green beans, or zucchini sticks.

Curry-in-a Hurry Dip

Makes 1½ cups dip.

One 8-ounce brick cream cheese,
  softened
½ cup sour cream or reduced-fat
  sour cream (a couple scoops)

1 rounded teaspoon curry powder
2 tablespoons honey (2 good
  drizzles)
6 pieces crystallized ginger, minced

Place all ingredients in a bowl. Combine with hand mixer on medium speed until smooth. Transfer to serving bowl and chill until ready to serve. Offer sliced green apples (soaked in a bit of lemon juice and water before plating to retard browning), blanched sugar snap peas, red pepper and seedless cucumber sticks.

The Ultimate Spinach Dip

Makes 2½ cups dip.

One 8-ounce brick cream cheese,
  softened
1 cup sour cream or reduced-fat sour
  cream (a couple good scoops)
1 packet vegetable soup mix (*not* the
  family size)

1 package (10 ounces) frozen
  spinach, defrosted and squeezed
  bone dry
1 can (8 ounce) sliced water chestnuts,
  drained and chopped
½ red bell pepper, finely diced

Combine everything in a bowl and stir it thoroughly. Dump this chunky dream into a serving dish and chill until ready to serve. Serve with carrot and celery sticks, red bell pepper strips, and blanched green beans. Or hollow out a small sourdough boule and fill bread with dip. Chop up bread top and serve along with veggies for dipping.

Close-to-Kim's Artichoke Dip

Makes 3¹/₂ cups dip.

1 can (15¹/₂ ounces) artichoke
hearts in water, drained and finely
chopped
2 cloves garlic, minced
1 cup mayonnaise or reduced-fat
mayonnaise

1 cup grated Parmigiano or Romano
cheese
8 ounces shredded mozzarella or
provolone cheese
A grind black pepper
2 pinches ground thyme

Combine all ingredients and bake until bubbly in 350°F preheated oven, about 20 minutes. Serve with shredded wheat crackers or garlic crostini (toasts).

VARIATION:

For spinach-artichoke dip, add 5 ounces drained and squeezed frozen chopped spinach (half a box) and substitute nutmeg for thyme.

One Cool Crab Dip

Makes 2 cups dip.

One 8-ounce brick cream cheese,
softened
¹/₂ cup sour cream or reduced-fat
sour cream
Juice of ¹/₂ lemon
12 blades fresh chives, chopped
Dash Tabasco sauce

¹/₄ red bell pepper, finely diced
2 cans (6¹/₂ ounces each) crabmeat, drained
A pinch coarse salt
A handful slivered almonds (available in small packets on baking
aisle), toasted till golden

Mix everything in bowl really well. Transfer to serving dish and chill until ready to serve. To serve, cover the top of serving dish with slivered toasted almonds and surround with melba toast and blanched snap peas, cauliflower florets, carrot and celery sticks, and red or yellow cherry tomatoes.

Spreads

Rumaki Spread

Makes 2½ cups spread.

3/4 stick (6 tablespoons) butter
2 large onions, thinly sliced
1 pound chicken livers, cleaned, trimmed and dried (This may require a shot of wine or other libation to execute.)
1 teaspoon salt (a quarter palmful)
1/4 teaspoon ground pepper (4 grinds or 2 pinches)

1/4 teaspoon ground thyme (a couple pinches)
6 slices center-cut bacon, cooked till crisp, crumbled
1 can (8 ounces) sliced water chestnuts, drained very well and chopped very fine

In a large skillet, melt butter over medium heat. Add onions and cook 10 minutes, stirring occasionally, until onions are soft and sweet. Add livers and sauté until cooked through and firm, about 12 to 15 minutes more. Cut through a liver to make sure no pink remains. Combine salt, pepper, and thyme in a small cup and sprinkle mixture over livers. Place contents of pan in blender or food processor and pulse until smooth paste forms. Chill until ready to serve. Set out 1 hour before serving and top with chestnuts and bacon. Surround spread with toasted, quartered, sliced white or wheat bread, melba toast, or pita cut into wedges and toasted in warm oven.

Marvelous Mac-a-Chut-Nut Cheese Spread

Makes 2¹/₂ cups spread.

1 small jar macadamia nuts
One 8-ounce brick cream cheese,
  softened
¹/₂ stick (4 tablespoons) butter,
  softened

1 package (10 ounces) sharp
  cheddar cheese, shredded
¹/₄ cup mango chutney
6 pieces crystallized ginger, minced,
  or 2 inches fresh gingerroot, grated

Grind nuts on Pulse in food processor and transfer to a small bowl. Cover and set aside. Fill processor with remaining ingredients and pulse until combined. Scrape with rubber spatula and transfer to serving bowl. Chill until ready to serve. Top with nuts and serve surrounded with sliced date-nut bread and halved mini-muffins from bakery section of market.

The Greatest of Garlic and Herb Spreads

Makes 2 cups spread.

(Make me a whole day ahead, I taste better that way.)

Two 8-ounce bricks cream cheese,
  softened
Juice of 1 lemon
2 cloves garlic, minced
¹/₂ small onion, peeled
4 leaves fresh sage, finely chopped

4 sprigs fresh thyme, leaves stripped
  and chopped
6 blades fresh chives, chopped
3 ounces toasted pine nuts, chopped
Cracked black pepper, to taste

Place cream cheese in a bowl. Squeeze lemon juice over it. Add garlic, then, with a hand grater, grate a small onion into bowl. Add sage and thyme and beat with hand mixer until creamy and smooth. Chill overnight. Bring back to room temperature to serve. Transfer to serving bowl and top with chives, toasted pine nuts, and cracked blacked pepper. Surround with lavash or or any other variety of flat bread, quartered slices of pumpernickel, or melba toasts.

Saltimbocca Spread

Makes 1 1/2 cups spread.

One 8-ounce brick cream cheese,
  softened
1/4 pound prosciutto di Parma,
  chopped
12 leaves fresh sage, piled on top of
  each other, then slivered

1 small onion, peeled
A splash heavy (whipping) cream or
  half-and-half
A few grinds black pepper
4 drops Worcestershire sauce

Place cream cheese in a bowl. Add prosciutto and sage. Grate the onion over bowl
with handheld grater. Add a splash of cream, pepper, and Worcestershire. Beat
with a wooden spoon until combined. Chill until ready to serve. Surround with
wine biscuits, water crackers, melba toast or crostini (little toasts).

Blue Cheese and Hazelnut Spread

Makes 2 cups spread.

1/4 pound Roquefort cheese
One 8-ounce brick cream cheese,
  softened

1 tablespoon Kirschwasser or other
  cherry liqueur
1/2 cup toasted chopped hazelnuts

Cream Roquefort, cream cheese, and Kirschwasser with a hand mixer. Transfer to
a smaller bowl and chill. Bring back to room temperature and combine half the
nuts with cheese mixture. Transfer to a serving bowl and top with remaining nuts.
Surround with sliced green apples and firm pears (set in lemon juice and water to
retard browning before plating), fresh split figs in season, and quartered sliced
canned brown bread with raisins.

Crushed Red Pepper Hummus

Makes 2 cups spread.

1 can (16 ounces) garbanzo beans,
   drained but with juice reserved
1/2 cup tahini paste (ground sesame
   paste, on natural foods aisle)
Juice of 1 lemon

2 cloves garlic, coarsely chopped
Two pinches coarse salt
3 pinches crushed red pepper flakes
Chopped parsley, for garnish

Combine all ingredients in food processor and pulse until paste forms. If the paste is too thick for your taste, add a little of the reserved juice to thin it. Transfer to a small bowl and cover tightly with plastic wrap. Sprinkle with parsley to serve and surround with lightly toasted pita wedges.

Deviled Egg Spread

Makes 2 cups spread.

12 large eggs
A pinch salt
1/2 small onion, peeled
1 teaspoon Dijon mustard
Mayonnaise or reduced-fat

mayonnaise to bind (1/3 to 1/2 cup)
4 drops Worcestershire sauce
A handful green pimiento-stuffed
   olives, chopped, for garnish
Assorted breads and celery sticks

Cover eggs with cold water and sprinkle in a little salt. Bring water to a boil, reduce heat to simmer and cook as close to 10 minutes as possible after water reaches boiling point. Run eggs under cold water to cool completely. Peel the eggs. Chop and place in a bowl. Mash eggs with a fork or a masher to a coarse mixture. Grate onion into bowl. Add Dijon, 4 tablespoons mayonnaise, and Worcestershire. Combine with a fork. If mixture seems dry, add more mayonnaise to reach desired consistency. Chill until ready to serve. Top with chopped green olives and surround with quartered pumpernickel, rye, marble, or sprouted wheat breads and sticks of celery heart.

Pick-Ups

Close-to-Grandma-Betar's Stuffed Grape Leaves

Makes 40 to 45 rolls.

One 8-ounce jar or tin grape leaves, drained
2 tablespoons extra-virgin olive oil (twice around the pan)
2 small cloves garlic, minced
1 medium onion, finely chopped
2 cups cooked long-grain white rice

4 sprigs fresh mint, finely chopped (2 tablespoons)
A palmful fresh dill, chopped (2 tablespoons)
Salt and pepper, to taste
6 ounces pine nuts (pignoli), toasted
Mint and dill sprigs, for garnish

Blanch drained leaves in simmering water for 15 to 20 seconds to separate leaves and remove brine. Drain, cool, and pat leaves dry.

Heat oil in a small skillet and cook garlic and onion over medium heat until tender. Remove from heat and combine with rice, mint, dill, salt and pepper, and half the pine nuts, chopped.

Place 2 teaspoons rice in center of leaf and roll, tucking in sides as you go. Place rolls tightly together in a skillet, making more than one layer if necessary, separating layers with leftover leaves. Barely cover leaves with simmering water. Place a plate on top of leaves and weight down with a couple of cans of canned goods. Simmer 30 minutes. Remove from heat and chill. To serve, dot with remaining nuts and small bouquet of mint and dill sprigs.

Meat-Filled Grape Leaves

Makes 40 to 45 rolls.

$^1/_2$ cup plain couscous

One 8-ounce jar grape leaves, leaves
blanched and dried as instructed
in preceding recipe

3 tablespoons extra-virgin olive oil
(3 times around the pan)

1 medium onion, finely chopped

2 cloves garlic, minced

1 pound ground lamb or veal

A palmful currants (3 or 4 tablespoons)

A palmful sliced almonds (3 or 4
tablespoons), available in small
pouches on baking aisle

2 or 3 pinches ground cinnamon
(about $^1/_4$ teaspoon)

2 or 3 pinches ground allspice

4 pinches curry powder

4 pinches paprika

Salt and ground black pepper, to
taste

A handful fresh mint leaves,
chopped (about 2 tablespoons)

A handful fresh flat-leaf parsley,
chopped (about 2 tablespoons)

Lemon wedges, for garnish

Prepare couscous according to directions on box and cool.

In a skillet, heat oil over medium heat and cook onion and garlic 5 minutes. Add lamb and cook another 5 minutes until browned. Remove from heat and stir in remaining ingredients. Wrap 2 teaspoons filling in each grape leaf and roll, tucking in sides as you go. Serve warm or cool with lemon wedges for garnish.

Spanikopita

Makes 36 spinach-and-feta triangles.

1 tablespoon extra-virgin olive oil
(once around the pan)

1 small onion, peeled and finely
chopped

8 ounces feta cheese, crumbled

1 large egg, beaten

2 pinches ground nutmeg

A few grinds black pepper

A palmful snipped fresh dill,
chopped (about 2 tablespoons)

A handful chopped fresh flat-leaf
parsley (about 2 tablespoons)

1 package (10 ounces) chopped
spinach, defrosted and squeezed
bone dry

$^1/_4$ stick (2 tablespoons) butter,
melted

12 sheets phyllo pastry dough
(from freezer section), defrosted

Heat olive oil over medium heat and cook onion until soft and sweet, about 5 minutes. In a bowl, combine crumbled feta cheese with nutmeg and pepper. Add dill, parsley, cooked onion, egg and spinach to feta mixture and toss together.

Place butter in small saucepan and melt.

Pile 12 sheets of pastry off to the side of your work surface. Keep pastry covered with damp paper towels. Pull out 1 sheet of pastry and brush with a light coat of butter. Top with a second sheet. Using a sharp knife, cut sheets in half across the middle. Cut each half into 3 equal strips. You should now have 6 strips, each a couple of inches wide. Place a couple of teaspoons of filling in lower left corner of first strip. Gently fold pile over, lining up bottom of strip with far edge of strip, hiding the filling under a triangle of dough. Continue crossing from side to side for 5 turns. Place your packet on an ungreased nonstick cookie sheet for immediate preparation, or in a shallow container if making ahead. Repeat process until you run out of pastry—you should have a yield of 36 pieces.

Cover and chill if making ahead. (These little puffs also freeze well.) When you are ready to serve, preheat oven to 400°F and bake until crisp and golden, 15 to 18 minutes.

Parmigiano Cheese Puffs

Makes 32 puffs.

1 cup milk
1 cup water
1 stick (8 tablespoons) butter
3 pinches coarse salt
1 cup all-purpose flour

8 large eggs
1 cup freshly grated Parmigiano
  cheese
2 or 3 pinches ground nutmeg
4 grinds black pepper

Preheat oven to 400°F.

In a saucepan combine milk, water, butter, and salt and bring to a boil over high heat. Reduce heat to medium and add the flour to pan. Stir with wooden spoon until mixture leaves the sides of pan and forms a big ball. Transfer to a mixing bowl and whisk in eggs, 2 at a time. After incorporating eggs, stir in Parmigiano, nutmeg, and pepper.

Make 16 mounds of rounded tablespoons of batter on buttered or nonstick baking sheet. Bake first set of puffs in upper third of oven at 400°F for 20 minutes, or until golden and crispy. Repeat with remaining batter.

Make a day ahead and store in airtight container until ready to serve. Yum!

Shrimp and Two Sauces

This allows 3 shrimps per person for 20 guests, as well as enough sauce to dip them in.

60 large cooked, cleaned, and
   deveined shrimp

ONE SAUCE
3/4 cup ketchup
1/4 cup mild chili sauce
1 tablespoon prepared horseradish
   (a scoop)

6 drops Worcestershire sauce
4 drops Tabasco sauce
2 stalks celery from tender heart,
   minced
Juice of 1/2 lemon
Snipped fresh chives or chopped
   fresh parsley, to garnish

Combine and chill until ready to serve.

TWO SAUCE
1 cup mayonnaise or reduced-fat
   mayonnaise
1/2 cup mild chili sauce
4 drops Worcestershire sauce

Salt and pepper, to taste
2 pinches Old Bay seasoning
1 shot (2 to 3 tablespoons) sherry
2 green onions, thinly sliced, for
   garnish
Lemon wedges (optional)

Combine all but green onions in bowl. Chill until ready to serve. Garnish this quick remoulade with green onions.

Serve your shrimp tails up, surrounding the two sauces. Place bowls for discards around the platter, along with a few lemon wedges for squirt-happy guests.

Clams Casino, Scorsese Style

Makes 24 clams.

As hot and fast as some of my favorite gangsters.

48 cherrystone clams
8 slices bacon, stacked and sliced
   into sixths, to yield 48 bacon
   pieces
1 1/2 sticks (12 tablespoons) butter,
   softened
4 cloves garlic, minced
A handful of fresh flat-leaf parsley,
   chopped (about 1/4 cup)
4 pinches crushed red pepper flakes
   (1/4 teaspoon)

6 drops Worcestershire sauce
A handful grated Parmigiano cheese
   (about 1/4 cup)
Bread crumbs
Lemon wedges and Tabasco sauce
   to serve

Coarse salt, sea or rock, to line
   baking sheet

Place clams in freezer for 15 minutes. Remove and pop open with small paring knife. Loosen clams on bottom half shell and set aside. Chuck the top shucked shells.

Preheat oven to 475°F.

Cook bacon pieces until fat is rendered but bacon is not yet crisp. Transfer to paper towel-lined plate to drain.

Spread a layer of coarse salt over the bottom of a cookie sheet or shallow pan; this will keep clams level as they bake.

Combine softened butter, garlic, parsley, crushed red pepper flakes, Worcestershire sauce, and cheese. Spread a slightly rounded teaspoon of spread over each clam and set shell into salt. Sprinkle each clam with bread crumbs and top with one bacon bit. Bake 10 minutes. Serve hot with lemon wedges and Tabasco sauce.

Bacon-Wrapped Scallops

Makes 40 pieces.

40 sea scallops, 2^1/$_4$ to 2^1/$_2$ pounds
20 slices lean, thinly sliced center-cut
  bacon
2 cans (8 ounces each) sliced water
  chestnuts, drained

1 teaspoon salt
^{1}/$_4$ teaspoon pepper (a few grinds)
^{1}/$_4$ teaspoon ground thyme or Old
  Bay seasoning (3 or 4 pinches)

Pat scallops dry on paper towels. Halve bacon slices. Place drained water chestnuts on a paper towel-lined plate. Combine salt, pepper, and thyme in a small ramekin or cup. Sprinkle mixture with fingers over scallops evenly, until seasoning blend is used up.

Top a seasoned scallop with a slice of chestnut. Roll in half a slice of bacon; repeat with each scallop. Chill until ready to serve.

Preheat broiler. Place scallops on a broiler pan, 20 at a time, and cook under preheated broiler until bacon is crisp. Repeat. Spear with toothpicks and transfer to platter.

Fig and Chicken Yakitori

Makes 20 pieces.

1^1/$_2$ to 2 pounds chicken tenders
  (20 pieces), halved (see Note,
  page 31)
^{1}/$_2$ cup Kikkoman or other good
  brand teriyaki sauce

2 tablespoons toasted sesame oil
5 fresh figs, quartered

20 bamboo skewers

Toss chicken pieces in teriyaki sauce. Heat 1 tablespoon sesame oil in skillet over medium-high heat till oil smokes. Cook half the chicken at a time for 6 to 8 minutes, until chicken is cooked through, giving the pan frequent shakes. Transfer to plate. Wipe out pan and return to heat. Repeat. When chicken is cool enough to handle, skewer 1 piece of chicken, followed by a quarter fig and a second piece of chicken. Serve at room temperature.

Peking Chicken Tenders

Makes 24 pieces

MARINADE
3 tablespoons toasted sesame oil
(3 times around the bowl)
3 tablespoons low-sodium soy sauce
(3 good splashes)
3 tablespoons rice wine vinegar
(3 good splashes)
3 cloves garlic, minced
4 pinches ground ginger or 2 inches
fresh gingerroot, grated
2 tablespoons dark brown sugar
Montreal Steak Seasoning (by
McCormick) or black pepper, to
taste

1³/₄ to 2 pounds chicken tenders
(see Note, page 31)

COATING
¹/₂ cup apricot all-fruit preserves
¹/₂ cup hoisin sauce (found on
Asian food aisle of market)

Toasted sesame seeds, a generous
sprinkling for garnish
2 green onions, thinly sliced, for
garnish

Bamboo party skewers for picking up

Mix marinade ingredients in a small bowl. Place tenders in a shallow baking dish and pour marinade over. Turn tenders in marinade and let stand 10 to 15 minutes for immediate use, or chill for up to 24 hours before using. Bring tenders back to room temperature before using.

Get a large skillet smoking hot over medium-high heat. Mix apricot preserves and hoisin sauce together while pan heats. Add half the tenders to hot pan, shaking off marinade as you pull from dish. Cook chicken 4 minutes on each side, giving the pan a good shake frequently. Baste with half the apricot coating. Cook another minute and, with a good shake and a strong arm, slide tenders across to a serving platter, glazed side up. Quickly rinse pan under hot water, wipe dry, and return to heat. Repeat. Sprinkle tenders with sesame seeds and green onions and serve with long bamboo skewers.

Pot Sticker Pork Pick-Ups

Makes 32 pieces.

These pork-burger sandwich pockets taste like a giant Chinese dumpling. Quartered, they become a reduced-fat, reduced-work, pot sticker dumpling for parties.

2 pounds ground pork
1/2 cup (a good handful) chopped
  water chestnuts
2 green onions, thinly sliced
3 tablespoons soy sauce (a couple
  good shakes)
1/2 teaspoon ground ginger
  (4 pinches) or 2 inches fresh
  ginger root, grated
2 cloves garlic, minced
A pinch crushed red pepper
1/2 orange (Grate the outer skin
  into bowl, then juice the orange
  into mixture.)

SALAD TOPPING
2 tablespoons honey (2 good
  drizzles)
1/2 cup white vinegar
1/2 European seedless cucumber,
  peeled, quartered, and thinly
  sliced
1 carrot, peeled and shredded

1 heart romaine lettuce, shredded

8 large flour tortilla wraps (1 package)
Hoisin sauce (available on the Asian
  foods aisle of the market)

Combine pork and next 7 ingredients in a bowl. Form into 8 thin patties and refrigerate until ready to use, up to 1 day ahead of serving.

Cook patties for 5 minutes on each side on nonstick skillet or grill pan over medium-high heat. Remove from heat and let stand.

Mix honey and vinegar and coat cucumber and carrot in the dressing. Shred romaine with sharp knife.

To heat wraps, get a big skillet or another griddle really hot and blister each tortilla for 15 seconds on each side, no oil necessary. Pile up cooked tortillas on a work surface.

To assemble, brush a tortilla with hoisin sauce. Top with a couple of scoops of cucumber and carrot salad, drained with a slotted spoon, a little shredded lettuce, and one pork pattie. Wrap tortilla up and over on all 4 sides and flip entire square-shaped packet over. Cut packets carefully from corner to corner. Stick a pick in the center of each of the 4 triangles and transfer to a serving dish.

They-Won't-Ever-Figure-It-Out Perfect Party Meatball

Makes 36 meat balls.

$^1/_2$ **cup falafel mix**
$^1/_4$ **cup water**
1 pound lean ground beef
2 cloves garlic, chopped
2 green onions, thinly sliced
A handful fresh flat-leaf parsley,
  chopped
2 pinches crushed red pepper flakes
2 tablespoons butter, softened

$^1/_2$ **teaspoon ground cumin**
  (4 pinches)
36 button mushroom caps
Coarse salt, to taste

4- to 6-inch bamboo skewers

1 jar (10 ounces) chili sauce or mild
  taco sauce, for dipping

Preheat oven to 450°F.

Mix falafel and water and let sit for 15 minutes. Combine with meat, garlic, green onion, parsley, and crushed red pepper. Form into 36 small balls and place on nonstick cookie sheet. Bake 10 minutes. Remove from oven.

Combine soft butter and cumin. Place this in a skillet and melt over medium heat. Sauté button mushroom caps until golden. Sprinkle with a little coarse salt.

Spear a mushroom, cap up, then a meatball. Surround a small bowl of chili sauce or taco sauce with meatballs.

Note: Balls can be made 24 hours ahead, chilled in airtight container overnight. Before serving, heat in a shallow baking dish at 325°F for 10 to 12 minutes.

Mamma's Stuffed Mushrooms

Makes 48 mushroom caps.

48 medium white mushrooms, cleaned with damp towel, stems removed, 12 reserved
1 tablespoon extra-virgin olive oil
1 tablespoon sherry or fresh lemon juice

STUFFING
1/2 stick (4 tablespoons) butter
2 tablespoons extra-virgin olive oil
1/2 red bell pepper, finely diced
4 cloves garlic, minced

12 mushroom stems, finely chopped
1 package (10 ounces) chopped frozen spinach, defrosted and squeezed bone dry
4 pinches ground nutmeg (about 1/4 teaspoon)
Coarse salt and black pepper, to taste
4 slices toasted white bread, finely diced
1 1/2 cups shredded fontina cheese (6 ounces)

We are going to precook the mushrooms to give them flavor and keep the stuffing from getting wet. Stuffed mushrooms are often either half raw and withered or so wet the stuffing slides off. Mamma knows how to get around that. God tells mammas just about everything; the rest they inevitably figure out themselves.

Sauté mushroom caps in olive oil over medium-high heat, shaking pan frequently, until juices are all extracted and have begun to evaporate (mushrooms at this stage are dark and tender and pan is nearly dry). Deglaze with a splash of sherry or lemon juice and keep pan on heat until liquid evaporates. Remove from stove and let cool to room temperature. Mushrooms, if necessary, may be stored at this stage for 24 hours in an airtight container.

To make stuffing, melt butter in oil in a large skillet over medium heat. Add red bell pepper, garlic, and mushroom stems and cook 3 to 4 minutes. Add spinach and sprinkle with nutmeg and salt and pepper to taste. Combine bread with spinach mixture and turn until bread absorbs all liquid. Remove from heat and let cool.

At this point stuffing may be stored for up to 24 hours ahead in a separate airtight container.

Once you are ready to stuff mushrooms, preheat oven to 400°F .

In a bowl, combine cheese and stuffing. Line up mushrooms on a small baking sheet or in shallow baking dish or dishes. Top each mushroom with a generous glob of stuffing, using fingertips and a teaspoon or a melon ball scoop.

Bake 12 to 15 minutes, or until golden. Serve hot.

Mamma, I love you.

Room-Temperature Entrées

These entrées—beef, pork, turkey, or fish—can travel from room to room with your party guests. Each recipe is designed to be eaten as a cocktail sandwich or, with a fork but no knife. **Each recipe feeds up to 20 as a party offering.**

Beef Tenderloin and Two Sauces

2 pieces beef tenderloin, center cut, no head or tail of loin, peeled of silver, skinned, and trimmed. (Ask your butcher to do this for you. If you know how to trim meat, let your pride take a vacation on this one. You need a total of about 4 pounds of the trimmed meat, or two 2-pound tenderloins.)

$1/4$ cup extra-virgin olive oil (a good drizzle for each loin)
Montreal Steak Seasoning (by McCormick) (available on the spice aisle—there is no real substitute.)

24 petit pain (small French bread rolls) or 4 baguettes, split and cut into 6 equal portions

ONE SAUCE

2 tablespoons prepared horseradish
1 tablespoon tarragon or white wine vinegar

$1/4$ onion, minced
1 cup sour cream or reduced-fat sour cream

Combine all ingredients well. Transfer to serving dish. May be made up to 48 hours in advance.

TWO SAUCE

$1/2$ cup sour cream or reduced-fat sour cream (3 or 4 heaped spoonfuls)
$1/2$ cup mayonnaise or reduced-fat mayonnaise (3 or 4 heaped spoonfuls)

2 rounded tablespoons Dijon mustard
2 tablespoons capers, smashed with flat of knife

Combine all ingredients well. Transfer to serving dish, or chill for up to 48 hours.

Coat meat with oil and crust with seasoning. Place on a rack in roasting pan.

Let meat sit, covered with plastic wrap, at room temperature for 30 minutes.

Place a rack in middle of oven and preheat oven to 400°F for 15 minutes.

Remove plastic wrap and place meat in hot oven. Roast 30 to 40 minutes and check temperature. For medium rare, take meat out at 135°F on meat thermometer. Meat will cook another 5 degrees, at least, as it rests. For medium well, take meat out at 150°F. Let meat rest under aluminum foil tent for 30 minutes to allow juices to fully distribute to safeguard against all of the flavor running out with the first slice.

Place meat on cutting board, sauces alongside, with teaspoons to serve. Slice 1 tender; leave 1 whole to slice as needed. Place a basket of split petit pain or baguettes alongside board for guests to build tiny meat sandwiches—a dripless delight.

Balsamic Pork Tenderloin

4 pounds trimmed pork tenderloins
Balsamic vinegar, a good splash
   per loin
Extra-virgin olive oil, a drizzle
   per loin
Montreal Steak Seasoning
   (by McCormick), to crust

1 cup sweet or hot Italian pickled
   pepper relish (found in Italian deli
   or condiment aisle)

A dish cornichon pickles to munch,
   alongside
24 petit pain, split, or 4 baguettes,
   split and cut into 6 portions

GARLIC AND HERB MAYONNAISE
1 cup mayonnaise or reduced-fat
   mayonnaise
4 sprigs fresh thyme, chopped
2 cloves garlic, minced
A few grinds black pepper

Preheat oven to 400°F.

Rub a splash of vinegar into each tenderloin. Coat tenderloins with a drizzle of extra-virgin olive oil—you need to coat the entire loin with a thin layer. Crust loins with seasoning. Place on rack in roasting pan. Roast at 400°F for 25 minutes, or until thermometer reads 155°F. Let meat rest 20 minutes, minimum, under aluminum foil tent.

Combine all ingredients for mayonnaise. Turn into a serving dish and have a teaspoon for portioning.

Slice half the meat and leave half whole for slicing as needed. Serve on cutting board with sweet and hot pepper relish and garlic mayonnaise. Set cornichons and basket of split breads alongside.

Elsa's Sliced Roast Salmon

1 side fresh Atlantic salmon, 2¹/₂
    to 3 pounds
Coarse salt
Juice of 1 lime
1 stick (8 tablespoons) butter, melted

A very sharp carving knife

SALMON SAUCE
1 cup sour cream or reduced-fat
    sour cream
2 tablespoons tarragon or white
    wine vinegar

A few fresh sprigs each, about 1
    tablespoon chopped, dill, chive,
    and tarragon
1 tablespoon capers, smashed with
    side of knife

A dish of peeled, thinly sliced
    European seedless cucumber, for
    stacking
12 slices pumpernickel bread,
    quartered into small squares for mini
    sandwich making, or 2 loaves
    cocktail-size sliced pumpernickel

Combine all ingredients for sauce in a bowl. Transfer to serving dish. Chill for up to 48 hours prior to party.

Cover bottom rack of your oven with aluminum foil.

Preheat oven to 400°F.

Rinse and dry salmon. Sprinkle with coarse salt. Place flesh side up in the middle of a carving board. With a very sharp carving or fillet knife, beginning at the tail end, slice salmon into ¹/₄-inch-thick slices at a steep angle, stopping each cut at skin. Do not cut through the skin, only *to* the skin. Flip carved meat over to the right as you slice, creating a fanlike effect.

Squeeze the juice of 1 lime into melted butter. Brush fish with mixture, allowing it to seep in and around the slices.

Turn a cookie sheet upside down. Oil flat surface of pan and carefully place fish on it. You need a pan with no lip whatsoever so that you may slide fish onto a serving platter or board without breaking once it's cooked. The aluminum foil covered bottom rack of oven will catch the runoff.

Roast on middle rack for 8 to 10 minutes, till thermometer reads 120°F, or until fish is firm and opaque.

Remove from oven and let cool. Carefully slide onto platter or board. Serve at room temperature with Salmon Sauce, sliced cucumbers, and split rolls. Cake servers or small spatulas make good utensils for serving fish. Small spatulas allow guests to lift salmon slices away from skin with ease.

Oven-Roasted Turkey Loco

1/2 stick (4 tablespoons) butter,
  softened
Juice of 2 limes
2 or 3 sprigs fresh oregano, finely
  chopped (about 1 tablespoon)
1 tablespoon ground cumin (half a
  palmful)
8 drops Tabasco sauce
1 full boneless turkey breast, 2
  pieces, totaling 4 to 4 1/2
  pounds (available in butcher case)

Coarse salt and black pepper,
  to taste

1 cup prepared green salsa (salsa
  verde), mild to medium, or 1 cup
  red chipotle salsa (smoky and
  hotter than green)
One 8-ounce brick cream cheese,
  softened
24 small cornmeal crusted rolls, split,
  or 12 mini pita pockets, halved

Preheat oven to 400°F.

Combine softened butter with lime juice, oregano, cumin, and Tabasco sauce. Rub breasts with mixture and place on rack in roasting pan. Cook 10 minutes at 400°F, then reduce to 350°F and roast another 45 minutes, basting frequently. After skin browns, place aluminum foil tent over breasts to keep skin from burning. Check internal temperature of turkey. It must read 180°F on meat thermometer at thickest part of breast before you can remove it from oven. Check every 10 to 15 minutes to reach this reading. Let breasts rest, then transfer to carving board.

Combine salsa and cream cheese to make a smooth spread. You can immediately serve or you can chill spread for up to 48 hours, then transfer to serving bowl and let stand till room temperature.

Slice 1 breast; reserve 1 for slicing as needed. Place the salsa spread out with a teaspoon for serving and a basket of split rolls or pita alongside.

Thai It, You'll Like It Sea Bass

A show-stopper.

1 farm-raised striped whole bass, 4
    pounds, cleaned
30 basil leaves (1 bunch of tops
    from produce department), picked
    from stems
1 lemon, thinly sliced
2 tablespoons extra-virgin olive oil
    (twice around the bowl in slow
    stream)
1 tablespoon toasted sesame oil
    (once around the bowl)
2 cloves garlic, minced
1 tablespoon soy sauce (a splash)
2 or 3 pinches crushed red pepper
    flakes
Freshly ground black pepper, to taste

THAI SALSA
1 peeled European seedless cucum-
    ber, halved and coarsely chopped
Coarse salt, to taste
2 pinches crushed red pepper flakes
A handful cilantro, chopped (about
    $1/4$ cup)
12 leaves basil, chopped
$1/4$ small red onion, finely chopped
$1/2$ small red bell pepper, finely
    diced
1 tablespoon honey (a good drizzle)
$1/4$ cup chopped peanuts (available
    on baking aisle)
2 tablespoons rice wine vinegar
    (2 splashes)
2 tablespoons vegetable or peanut oil

Preheat oven to 350°F.

Pat fish dry, inside and out. Fill the fish with basil and lemon slices in an even layer. Combine oils, garlic, soy sauce, and red pepper flakes. Coat fish with this dressing using brush. Pour any excess inside the cavity. Grind pepper over fish. Place fish on oiled shallow pan and bake 50 to 60 minutes.

Transfer fish to board. With a sharp knife, break the skin along the backbone. Cut first side of fish in 2-inch strips, through the meat and down to the bone. Let guests remove slices with spatula, telling them to gently ease meat away from the bone. Chunky salsa placed alongside fish in small serving bowl is for topping fish.

Remove the spine and bones, and the basil and lemon, to expose the bottom half of fish. Chunk with a spatula and a knife. This is messier than the rest of the room temperature entrées because you need to offer forks and you must remove the fish's spine, but boy, will you be popular when everyone eats.

Pecan-Crowned Brie

Place a whole half kilo brie, 1.1 pounds, in a 10-inch round baking dish. Spread top of brie with apricot all-fruit preserves warmed in microwave to thin for spreading. Arrange whole pecan halves (about 1 cup) in tight circular pattern on top of brie, working from center out. Bake at 350°F in center of oven for 12 minutes, or just until cheese begins to melt. Set out on warming tray or at room temperature (it will retain heat for a while) and serve with sliced apples and pears (see Note) and sesame bread sticks for dipping. Garnish with edible flowers, available in produce department near herbs.

Note: Turn apple and pear slices in lemon juice and water before plating to retard browning.

AUTHOR'S NOTE:
An afternoon at Paumanok.

On the north fork of Long Island there lies a community of vintners producing some of the world's finest wines. It's a fairly new community of very entrepreneurial people—professionals of all kinds turned farmers.

Charles Massoud, one of the people in this community, was an IBM executive, and happy as such. But one day Charles looked around and started to notice those men ten to fifteen years his senior. He recognized something very clearly. "The flame had gone out of their lives. That's how I would end up. You don't appreciate that when you are young."

Charles and his wife, Ursula, as loving as she is strong, took a patch of land and built a new life for their young family. They walked away from a corporate dream into something they hoped would turn out to be a fairy tale.

A fairy tale it is. A little romance as well . . . Ursula recalls the early days when Charles was moonlighting in the young vineyards, ". . . coming out on Friday night in his very chic suit and tie only to get on the tractor the next morning in his old jeans and boots; I discovered a side to him I never knew he had."

I have rarely been so wholly content as when sitting at the kitchen table with the Massouds—Charles, Ursula, and middle son, Karim, listening to stories about family, faith, and grapevines. You can taste the work, the love, in every delicious drop of Paumanok wines.

The food we ate had the same depth. Aldo, a friend, a cook, "a true artist," says Charles, created a wonderful selection of hearty foods presented so well that at meal's end we were left satisfied and very, very happy.

**For an intimate gathering of six to ten, this simple menu is
all anyone could ever want.**

Aldo's Cold Herb-Roasted Chicken and
Blanched Green Beans with Parsley

Aldo's Loin of Lamb with Lentils
Assorted mustards and multigrain breads

Paumanok Merlot

Assorted soft French cheeses such as Crotin, Robouchon, Brie
Late Harvest riesling
Aldo's Almond Biscotti

In my own ode to Aldo, I've attempted to figure out the chicken and the lamb. But
you'll have to consult your best Italian bakery for a reproduction of his master-
piece, the perfect almond biscotti. I have never been able to bake, and have twice
as little advice on this twice-baked delight.

I hope you enjoy this menu for many years with your best of friends. I also hope
you travel to the North Fork of Long Island to see the Paumanok vineyards your-
selves. The Massouds are too wonderful to miss; they're good-friends-in-waiting.

This is a cold meal, brought to room temperature to serve, and can be prepared
in its entirety a day ahead.

Aldo's Cold Herb-Roasted Chicken and Blanched Green Beans with Parsley

2 small young chickens, cut up by butcher—breasts, thighs, legs, 12 pieces total (Use backs and wings for another use—soup, stock, etc.)
Extra-virgin olive oil
1 teaspoon coarse salt
1/4 teaspoon black pepper

1 teaspoon dried herbes de Provence seasoning blend (parsley, sage, rosemary, thyme)

1 1/2 pounds green beans
A drizzle extra-virgin olive oil
A pinch coarse salt
A few sprigs fresh flat-leaf parsley, chopped (about 1 tablespoon)

Preheat oven to 400°F.

Wash and pat chickens dry. Coat chickens lightly with olive oil. Combine salt, pepper, and herbs in a small dish. Rub seasoning into the skin of chicken pieces. Arrange chicken on a rack in roasting pan in a single layer. Place in the center of oven and reduce heat to 350°F. Roast chicken 30 to 40 minutes, depending on size of pieces, basting every 15 minutes. Place aluminum foil tent over top of pan once skin begins to brown to keep it from becoming too dark. Remove chicken from oven when meat thermometer reads 165°F, or when juices run clear when skin is pricked at deepest part of thigh.

Bring chicken to room temperature before lifting to a plate or storage container.

To prepare beans, add just enough water to cover the bottom of a skillet. Set beans in pan and bring to a boil. Reduce heat to lowest setting, cover, and steam 3 minutes. Drain beans in colander and run under cool water. Pat beans dry and transfer to a shallow bowl. Drizzle beans with a little extra-virgin oil and sprinkle with just a touch of coarse salt and a little parsley. Beans can be stored in fridge in airtight container; bring back to room temperature before serving.

To serve, arrange chicken down the center of a long oval platter and surround with blanched beans.

Aldo's Loin of Lamb with Lentils

Two 14- to 16-ounce pieces boned loins of lamb from your butcher's counter
Extra-virgin olive oil
Coarse salt
1 pound dried brown lentils
A sprinkle coarse salt
1/3 cup extra-virgin olive oil (a good couple of glugs)

Juice of 1/2 lemon
A quarter palmful ground cumin (1 teaspoon)
A few grinds black pepper
A palmful very finely minced fresh parsley or mint (about 2 table-spoons)

Dijon mustard and crusty, multi-grain bread for serving

Preheat oven to 400°F.

Coat each loin with a drizzle of olive oil and sprinkle with a pinch of salt. Heat a skillet over medium-high heat. Place loins in very hot pan and cook 1 minute, sautéing on all sides. Place aluminum foil over pot handle to keep it from burning and transfer pan to oven. Cook 7 to 8 minutes, removing when thermometer reads 145° to 150°F for medium.

Let meat come to room temperature. Store, covered, in fridge until ready to serve. Bring back to room temperature. Slice lamb into 1/4-inch-thick rounds and fan out down half of a long oval platter, saving space for lentil salad alongside. Serve meat with Dijon mustard and sliced multi-grain crusty bread (Aldo made that, too).

To prepare the lentils, place them in a small pot and add enough tap water to just cover. Place the pot on the stove and bring the water to a boil, reduce heat to a simmer, and cook 25 minutes, or until lentils are just tender. While they cook, combine oil, lemon juice, cumin, pepper, and minced parsley or mint in the bottom of a large bowl. Drain lentils well and immediately transfer to bowl with dressing. Toss until warm lentils absorb dressing. Season with salt, to taste. Serve at room temperature.

At Home Sundays

Breakfast, Lunch, and Sunday Suppers

Sundays with Zia Patrina

When Zia Patrina came to town with uncle Jimmy (Vincenzo before Ellis Island), the ten kids, my mother the eldest, would come running to gather 'round. Every month-long summer visit meant fun and good food—a month of Sundays, literally. Each day the kids would swim and fish and play at the feet of the men. The brothers—Jimmy, Emery, Henry, and John (Vincenzo, Emmanuel, Nunzio, and Nicolo)—would visit for hours with the Runzo boys, the three clowns. They would tell endless stories, play cards, and roast chestnuts over small campfires. They would break up the day with a row in the boat or a nap in the hammocks.

Zia always insisted on cooking. She was a six-foot-tall Calabrese woman and no one argued with Zia Patrina. She would always do as she pleased, and it pleased her to take over the house. The kids loved her. She let them make fun of her at breakfast, when she preferred to eat pasta, not eggs. She would teach them Italian rhymes and games while preparing the food in the afternoons. Zia Patrina always wore a long apron from which she hung her *moppines* (slang for kitchen rags). With her brightly colored towels streaming from her waistband, Zia looked like a gypsy queen.

At the day's end, everyone gathered around the table and dove into a feast— kettles of crackling shrimp in garlic and oil, eggplant, pasta, greens. Whatever filled the big black roasting pan was the favorite that night—meat with potatoes, onion, tomato, and cheese, whole fish cooked in wine and garlic, or Zia's famous chicken. The table was quiet only long enough to swallow. Everyone chattered and visited, like a gaggle of geese, for hours.

After the meal, Henry, who fancied himself a Jimmy Durante ("Ha-cha-cha" was his most common expression), would pick up his *accordine*, his squeeze box, and Patrina the gypsy queen would come to life! She'd pull the *moppines* from her waist and twirl them above her head, leading the children in the tarantella, the music and movements so passionate that even the fireflies danced. What fun they all had.

—RACHAEL RAY

Sundays

As a child I awoke on Sundays to the smell of pork and garlic in the frying pan—the prelude to my father's spaghetti sauce.

At noon we sat down with my aunt and uncle to eat, but invariably company would arrive unannounced, more uncles and aunts and cousins from a city seventy-five miles away. There was always enough food to go around, and soon the table was a cacophony of animated voices vying amicably for attention. Meanwhile my mom heaped on seconds of meatballs and pasta and sausage and pork.

Then came the main course and side dishes—chicken with rosemary potatoes, roast beef, beans, peas, and then salad. After the fruit, women retired to the next room to gossip, the men played cards, every so often calling me to draw more wine from the barrels downstairs.

We played outside, running in to grab more food, but by late afternoon or early evening, there we all were again, at the table eating leftovers. After my mother served coffee and dessert I was allowed to sip some of the adults' anisette. It all felt so good. And it feels wonderful now to recall the sights and sounds and smells of those Sundays—they will stay with me forever.

—Dan DiNicola

Breakfast

Homemade Sunday Sausage Patties

Makes 8 large patties or 12 to 16 mini patties.

1 1/2 pounds ground pork
1 teaspoon (4 pinches) ground
 ginger or 2 inches peeled and
 freshly grated gingerroot
1 teaspoon fennel seed (measured
 in the palm of your hand)

1/2 teaspoon (2 pinches) allspice
Coarse salt and ground pepper,
 to taste
1 tablespoon vegetable oil (once
 around the pan)

Combine pork and seasonings very thoroughly and form into patties. Heat lightly greased skillet or griddle pan over medium-high heat. Cook sausage patties until brown on each side, about 7 or 8 minutes total. Place in oven on Warm until ready to serve.

Brown Sugar and Black Pepper Bacon

Feeds 8.

1 pound peppered bacon, sliced
 (available in custom meat or retail
 case of your market)

3 tablespoons (a handful) dark
 brown sugar

Preheat oven to 375°F.

Place bacon on broiler pan on center rack of oven. Cook 8 to 10 minutes, then remove from oven. Sprinkle bacon with sugar and return to oven. Cook another minute or two until bacon is a dark reddish brown and crisp. Remove and serve warm.

Red-Eye Ham

Feeds up to 8.

Two $3/4$ to 1 pound cooked ham steaks
2 pats (2 tablespoons) butter or
margarine
$1/2$ cup strong coffee

Remove ham from package and pat dry with paper towels. Heat a big nonstick skillet over medium-high heat. To a hot pan, add a pat of butter or margarine. As soon as it melts, it will begin to smoke. Add 1 ham steak and cook 3 or 4 minutes on each side. Add half the coffee and deglaze the pan, rubbing the ham steak around the pan and turning once to pick up color and coffee glaze. When coffee has evaporated, remove ham and place on plate to keep in a warm oven until you are ready to serve. Wipe pan clean and repeat process with second ham steak.

Broiled Half Grapefruits

8 servings.

4 large ruby red grapefruits, halved
across the middle and sectioned
$1/2$ cup dark brown sugar

Arrange sectioned grapefruits on a cookie sheet and coat each top with about a tablespoon of brown sugar. Place under preheated broiler and broil until sugar melts and turns golden and bubbly. Simple and simply yummy.

Melon and Milk Bowls

Makes 8 bowls.

These are perfect for hot summer Sundays.

4 ripe cantaloupes, halved across
the belly and seeded with a large
spoon

8 scoops vanilla ice cream or ice milk
$1/2$ pint raspberries, blackberries,
or blueberries, for garnish

Fill cold, seeded half melon bowls with a scoop of ice milk or frozen yogurt and top with a few berries of choice. Serve with big spoons that make you open wide—with this refreshing dish, the bigger the bite, the greater your delight!

Drunken Grapefruit Salad

8 servings.

2 quarts fresh grapefruit sections
   (available in refrigerated case of
   produce departments)

1/4 cup sugar
3 ounces gin
16 leaves fresh mint

Drain grapefruit, reserving juice, and place in a bowl. Pour about 1/2 cup of reserved juice over grapefruit and sprinkle with sugar; mix until sugar dissolves. Place the sections in 8 serving cups. Pour a splash of gin over each dish, about 1 teaspoon. Pile 8 mint leaves on top of each other and roll into a log. Slice log into slivers and sprinkle each cup with mint threads. Garnish each cup with 1 of the remaining leaves and serve immediately. WOW, is this stuff good!

Savory Scrambled Eggs

Feeds 8.

20 large eggs
A splash cold water (I don't know why,
   Grampa just did it that way.)
2 pats (2 tablespoons) cold butter, cut
   into tiny bits
4 sprigs fresh tarragon (about 2
   tablespoons), chopped

10 blades fresh chives, finely chopped
Freshly ground black pepper, to taste
2 or 3 pinches coarse salt, plus a
   pinch over your left shoulder
   for luck
1 pat (1 tablespoon) butter, for
   cooking

Crack the eggs into a large bowl and beat with a wire whisk for 3 minutes. Add just a splash of very cold water and bits of butter to beaten eggs. Toss in tarragon, chives, pepper, and a little salt. Whisk briefly to combine.

Heat a big nonstick skillet over medium-low heat. Brush pan with a touch of butter nested in a paper towel.

Add eggs and cook, stirring with a wooden spoon, until eggs reach desired consistency for your crowd. At my house, eggs have to come out of the pan in stages—Pop likes them soft enough to suck through a straw, my brother likes anything exactly the opposite of however you cooked it, Mom never eats, "she'll just pick," and my sister Maria likes them "dead" or cooked until they are unrecognizable as eggs (she also puts mayonnaise on French toast). They say there is one in every family—we have five. Thank God for my dog, Boo.

Potato Pancakes

Serves 8.

1 sack (20 ounces) shredded Simply
   Potatoes (found on dairy aisle, near
   eggs)
1 large onion, peeled and grated with
   hand grater
Montreal Steak Seasoning (by
   McCormick) or coarse salt and

black pepper, to taste
A few pinches paprika
2 large eggs, separated and each
   beaten well (whites into soft peaks)
2 tablespoons all-purpose flour
   (a palmful)
Butter for greasing griddle

Dump potatoes in a bowl. Place grated onion on double layer of paper towels. Pull up edges like a pouch and squeeze liquid out of onion. Add onion to potatoes. Add seasonings, beaten egg yolks, and flour. Mix well, then fold in fluffy beaten egg whites.

Grease griddle pan with butter nested in paper towel, then place pan on moderate heat. Place a couple of tablespoons of potato mixture in 4 piles on pan and flatten. Cook cakes till edges are golden. Flip and brown the other sides. Remove to 200°F oven to keep warm until ready to serve; repeat process with next batch of potato mixture.

This is yummy with gobs of applesauce on top. Or, for a change, mix whole berry cranberry sauce with applesauce in a 1 to 1 ratio for a fall-colored potato pancake topping.

Frittatas: Big Egg Pies

B.L.T. Frittata

Serves up to 8.

2 bunches arugula, a.k.a. "rocket lettuce," chopped (about 2 cups)

$1/2$ pound pancetta or center-cut bacon, chopped

6 fresh, firm plum tomatoes

20 large eggs

2 tablespoons cold butter, cut into tiny bits

A splash very cold water

Coarse salt and black pepper, to taste

2 tablespoons extra-virgin olive oil (twice around the pan)

4 cloves garlic, minced

1 pat (1 tablespoon) butter, for cooking

Wash arugula well. If it is especially sandy, let it soak in a bowl of cold water till sand settles to bottom of bowl. Dry greens gently on paper towels. Coarsely chop dried greens and set aside.

Brown chopped pancetta or bacon over moderate heat and transfer to a paper towel–lined plate.

Heat a small saucepan filled with water to a boil. Split the skins of tomatoes with a shallow X on both ends and drop tomatoes in water for 30 seconds to loosen skins. Remove tomatoes and peel away skins under running water. Halve tomatoes with a paring knife and let seeds fall into sink. Pat peeled, seeded tomatoes with paper towel. Dice tomatoes and set aside.

Beat eggs with a whisk for 3 minutes. Add butter bits, a splash of cold water, and salt and pepper.

Heat your largest nonstick skillet over medium heat. Add olive oil and garlic and cook until the garlic speaks by sizzling gently in oil. Add arugula and sauté in garlic oil for 2 or 3 minutes.

Nest a pat of butter in paper towel and run it around the sides of the skillet.

Add eggs to pan and gently stir with wooden spoon until eggs begin to set. Stir in pancetta or bacon bits and tomato.

Stop stirring but continue to cook, gently lifting cooked egg up from bottom with a spatula, allowing liquids to settle, until this big omelet is firmly set. Place pan on center rack of oven and broil until top is golden brown. Leave oven door ajar if the handle of pan is not ovenproof. Cut browned egg pie into 8 wedges and serve warm.

Swiss Chard and Potato Frittata

Feeds 8.

3 tablespoons butter
2 tablespoons vegetable oil (twice
   around the pan)
1 pouch (20 ounces) shredded Simply
   Potatoes (Found near eggs on dairy
   aisle of market—boy, do these save
   a lot of time.)

1 medium onion, chopped
Coarse salt and black pepper, to taste
1 bunch Swiss chard, stems removed,
   washed, drained, dried, and
   coarsely chopped
16 large eggs
2 pinches ground nutmeg

Heat a large nonstick skillet over medium-high heat. Melt butter in oil and add shredded potatoes and onion. Cook potatoes for 8 to 10 minutes, turning only occasionally. Potatoes should be lightly browned. If potatoes are getting too dark on edges, reduce heat a little. Sprinkle with salt and pepper.

While potatoes cook, place chard in a second smaller skillet and add a cup or so of water to pan. Bring to a boil, cover, and steam 5 minutes or so. Dump chard into colander and allow them to drain and cool.

Beat eggs for 3 minutes with the 2 pinches of nutmeg. Turn browned potatoes, making sure they are not sticking to the pan in any one area. Pour eggs over potatoes. Reduce heat to medium low. Go to sink and squeeze out your chard. Sprinkle chard over the eggs and combine gently. Continue to cook, lifting up set egg from bottom to allow liquids to settle until frittata becomes firm. Place in center rack of oven and broil until top is evenly golden brown. Cut into 8 wedges and serve warm.

Fennel, Onion, and Fontina Frittata

Feeds 8.

2 tablespoons butter
2 tablespoons extra-virgin olive oil
1 bulb fresh fennel, top trimmed
   away, bulb halved and thinly
   sliced

1 large sweet onion, Spanish or Vidalia,
   peeled, halved, and thinly sliced
18 large eggs
Coarse salt and black pepper, to taste
1/2 pound fontina cheese, well chilled,
   then sliced

Heat a large nonstick skillet over medium heat. Melt butter in oil, then add fennel and onion to pan. Cook 15 to 20 minutes, stirring frequently, until onion and fennel caramelize or turn golden brown and are sweet to the taste.

While fennel and onions cook, beat eggs with a whisk for 3 minutes. Season with salt and pepper.

Pour eggs over fennel and onion and cook until eggs are firmly set, lifting up set egg from bottom occasionally to allow liquids to settle. When frittata is firm, place on center rack in oven and broil until top begins to brown. Cover top with fontina slices and place back under broiler till cheese just melts. Cut into 8 wedges and serve warm.

Rosemary Hash Browns

Makes 8 servings.

2 tablespoons butter

2 tablespoons extra-virgin olive oil

1 pouch (20 ounces) shredded Simply Potatoes (found near eggs on dairy aisle)

1 medium onion, peeled

4 sprigs fresh rosemary, leaves stripped from stems (about 2 tablespoons)

Montreal Steak Seasoning (by McCormick) or coarse salt and black pepper, to taste

Melt butter in oil in a medium nonstick frying pan over medium to medium-high heat. Add potatoes to pan. Take onion in hand and using a hand grater and working over the pan, grate onion into potatoes. Brown potatoes and onion until golden, 10 to 12 minutes. Add rosemary and seasoning. Cook another minute or two and serve warm.

The King of the Corned: A Heavenly Hash

Feeds 8, well.

1/2 pound peppered bacon (from butcher counter) or pancetta, chopped

1 sack (20 ounces) diced Simply Potatoes with onion, removed from bag and coarsely chopped to half the original size

2 pounds sliced cooked corned beef, chopped

1 large yellow-skinned onion, minced

A shot good bourbon

4 shakes Worcestershire sauce

3 or 4 pinches ground nutmeg

2 pinches ground cloves

Freshly ground black pepper, to taste

1 tablespoon vegetable oil (once around the pan)

1 cup heavy (whipping) cream or half-and-half

A handful fresh flat-leaf parsley, chopped

8 jumbo eggs

Cook bacon in small skillet and drain on paper towels. Combine everything except oil, cream, parsley, and eggs in a big bowl. Heat oil in the bottom of a big, heavy-bottomed skillet over medium heat until pan begins to smoke. Add hash mixture and press down all over with a spatula. Cook 15 minutes, turning and pressing down as it crusts on bottom.

While hash cooks, reduce cream by half, simmering it in a small saucepan. Mix in cream and turn through hash. Turn heat down and cook until the bottom crusts.

Preheat broiler so you can crust the top of hash when done.

Prepare 8 eggs as you like—fried, over, sunnyside up or poached.

Brown top of hash pan under broiler till crusty, then top with parsley. Add eggs to top of pan carefully. Serve with toasted "sandwich-size" plain or sourdough English muffins.

The Finest French Toasts

Pain Perdu: Lost Bread

Makes 8 slices.

The original French toast. "Lost" bread refers to stale bread, the texture lost but brought back to life with custard batter.

2 jumbo eggs
1 cup sugar (No, it's not a misprint.)
1 tablespoon cornstarch
2 or 3 drops vanilla extract
1 cup milk or low-fat milk
2 or 3 pinches ground nutmeg

Butter, to grease skillet
1 loaf stale challah, ends cut off and
    sliced into 8 even slices
Powdered sugar or maple syrup, to top

Beat eggs 2 to 3 minutes with an electric mixer. Add the sugar and continue to beat. Add cornstarch and vanilla and beat in. When well mixed, add milk and nutmeg and mix well again. Pour batter into pie dish.

Heat a griddle or skillet over medium heat. Rub griddle with a touch of butter. Dip stale bread in batter and coat each side well. Cook slices until golden brown on each side and serve with a sprinkle of powdered sugar or warm maple syrup.

Toast Tips

If your doctor has threatened you into watching your cholesterol, like my friend Frank, substitute two large egg whites for each large egg.

For most toast recipes, you can make a double batch when you are feeling ambitious. French toast freezes really well. Just wrap them individually and pop them in the toaster whenever you get the urge (you can finally leggo those Eggos.)

To keep toast warm while preparing a large batch, place on a plate in a warm oven. NEVER microwave bread unless you enjoy the texture of shoe leather.

No-Pain Pain au Chocolat

8 to 10 servings.

If you have neither the time nor the aptitude for making chocolate croissants (pain au chocolate), this rich treat will fill the craving and then some.

1 recipe Pain Perdu batter (page 86)
10 slices firm white toasting bread,
**   crusts trimmed**

6 ounces bittersweet chocolate (from
**   baking bars)**
Butter, for frying
Powdered sugar or powdered cocoa,
**   for topping**

Pour enough batter to coat a 9 by 13-inch baking dish with a 1/8-inch layer of liquid. Place 5 slices of bread in the dish. Scatter bits of chocolate on bread, leaving a 1/2-inch border around edge of bread. Place 5 more slices of bread on top, making a chocolate sandwich. Pour the rest of batter down and over sandwiches. Lift completed sandwiches out of liquid and onto a plate so they do not get too soggy. Cook sandwiches 2 or 3 at a time on a lightly greased nonstick skillet or griddle pan over medium heat until golden and crisp on both sides. Keep sandwiches warm in low-temperature oven on a cookie sheet till all sandwiches are fried. When you are ready to serve, cut sandwiches from corner to corner diagonally. Gently separate sandwiches and arrange on serving dish. Sprinkle with a little powdered sugar or powdered cocoa.

VARIATIONS

Mocha Bread

Use 1/4 cup strong black coffee plus 3/4 cup milk in Pain Perdu batter. Proceed with above method.

Berry-Stuffed French Toast

If chocolate is not a morning taste for your mouth, substitute sliced strawberries or a few blackberries or raspberries, adding them at the same stage in Pain Perdu recipe as chocolate bits. Proceed with the method as written.

Morning Monte Cristos

Makes 5 sandwiches.

1 recipe Pain Perdu batter (page 86)
10 slices firm white toasting bread,
 crusts trimmed
5 teaspoons all-fruit apricot jam
10 thin slices Golden Delicious apple

5 slices baked ham (from the deli
 counter)
One 8-ounce brick smoked cheddar
 cheese, thinly sliced
Butter, for frying
Powdered sugar, for topping

Pour 1/8 inch batter into a 9 by 13-inch baking dish. Spread 5 slices bread with 1 teaspoon apricot jam each and set them, jam side up, in dish. Top each with 2 thin slices of apple, a slice of ham folded to fit bread, and a thin layer of smoked cheddar cheese. Top with remaining 5 slices bread and pour the rest of the batter over the tops of the sandwiches. Lift sandwiches out of batter and transfer to a dish to keep bread from getting too soggy. Fry sandwiches in a lightly greased nonstick skillet over medium heat until golden on each side, adding a little butter to pan as needed. Keep sandwiches in low-temperature oven till all are completed. Cut sandwiches in half diagonally and arrange on platter. Sprinkle with a touch of powdered sugar and serve warm.

Pancakes

Country Flapjacks

Feeds 6 to 8.

3 cups all-purpose flour
3 tablespoons sugar
2 tablespoons baking powder
1/2 teaspoon salt

6 eggs, beaten
2 1/2 cups half-and-half
6 tablespoons butter, melted

Always sift your flour and any other dry ingredients into a bowl to begin. This makes lighter pancakes. I don't like using a traditional sifter—I make a big mess getting the flour into it. I place a wire strainer over a big bowl with the handle hanging out over the side. I dump all the dry ingredients into the strainer, pick up the handle, and knock the side of the strainer with my free hand till it's empty.

Make a well in the center of dry ingredients. Mix the liquids, starting with beaten egg and adding the remaining liquids to that. Dump the mixed liquids into the well and beat until batter is just mixed. This is for big, fluffy, American-style flapjacks. If you overmix the batter, you thin the pancake—the result is a crepe, not a flapjack.

Cook pancakes over only moderate heat. Brush pan with a touch of butter nested in paper towel. Cook pancakes until bubbles pop up all across the top of batter and edges are golden brown. The flip side of cake will take only a minute or so to cook and turn golden.

A couple tablespoons of batter will make a nice 4- to 5-inch cake. Go smaller with 1 tablespoon for silver dollar cakes, 1 tablespoon larger for hungry-man cakes.

Happy Cakes are cool for kids. Make two eyes and a mouth shape on griddle with teaspoons of batter and let cook for 30 seconds. Spoon three tablespoons more batter over eyes and mouth to form "head". Flip when head is covered with bubbles and edges are golden.

VARIATIONS

Pecan or Hazelnut Pancakes

Place 1 cup whole or halved nuts in a plastic food storage bag and whack with a blunt instrument—meat mallet, flat iron, whatever is handy. Place dazed nuts in a cake pan and roast 'n toast for 10 minutes in 300°F oven to release flavors. Sprinkle batter with toasted nuts just after adding it to skillet.

Banana Nut Pancakes

Add two or three thin slices of ripe banana to cakes when you sprinkle with nuts.

Pancake Pointers

Preheat oven to 200°F before you begin any pancake recipe. Put a dinner plate in there so you can keep transferring the cakes as you flip through a whole batch of batter. Keep a loose aluminum foil tent over the plate to keep cakes from drying out on top.

Warm your syrup. You'll use less and it will taste better. Put the syrup in a serving bowl or pitcher and place it in the oven with your pancake plate before you start recipe.

Don't waste your money on flavored syrups. Drop a little cinnamon oil, vanilla, or mushed blackberries into syrup as you are pouring it into pitcher or serving bowl. Place it in a warm oven while preparing your pancakes and the heat will infuse the syrup with the flavor of whatever you put in it.

Chocolate Chip Pancakes

Sprinkle mini semisweet morsels on pancakes just before flipping from side 1 to side 2.

Blueberry Corn Pancakes

There is no better cornmeal pancake recipe than the one on the side of the Jiffy corn muffin mix box. For 6 to 8 people, buy three boxes. (Less is never more when you're talking breakfast.) Follow, to the letter, the directions on the box for the pancake batter adaptation. Sprinkle corn cakes with ripe fresh blueberries just before flipping.

Belgian Waffles

Makes 16 4-inch waffles.

3 $1/3$ cups all-purpose flour
$1/4$ cup sugar
1 tablespoon plus 1 teaspoon baking
   powder
1 teaspoon salt

3 $3/4$ cups cold low-fat milk
6 tablespoons butter, melted
3 jumbo eggs
Cooking spray

Dump everything in a big bowl and mix until smooth. Let the batter rest 10 minutes before you use it.

Open hot waffle iron and lightly spray it, top and bottom, with cooking spray.

Place 1 to 1 $1/2$ cups batter at a time into your waffle iron, spreading it out evenly with a plastic spatula. Allow batter to bubble up, then close waffle iron and set its timer or cook until your indicator light comes on.

Cherry-Berry Garnishes

For the edge of any Sunday breakfast plate, dip the tips of large, sweet Driscoll long stem strawberries in a bowl of cherry pie filling to coat. A glossy, simple tasty treat for one and all. Way more exciting than half an orange slice and a piece of wilted kale.

VARIATIONS

Nut Waffles

Stir 3/4 cup crushed toasted pecans, walnuts, or filberts into batter.

Chocolate Chip Waffles

Sprinkle a palmful of chips over batter after adding it to waffle iron.

Blueberry Waffles

Sprinkle a handful of berries evenly over batter just before closing waffle iron.

Kirschwasser Waffles

Use 1/4 cup less milk and add 1/4 cup kirsch and 2 tablespoons orange zest to basic recipe for a real cherry of a waffle.

Waffle Tips

Get your waffle iron really hot before adding batter. If you have a waffle iron with a thermostat, place it on medium-high setting and let it warm for ten to fifteen minutes before using.

Waffles freeze well. Individually wrap them and pop them in the toaster as needed.

Don't make everyone wait to eat the waffles. Waffles are best and crispiest right out of the waffle iron. Let each person dig right in as the waffles are ready. If you have separation anxiety, let everyone eat in the kitchen at the counter or take the waffle iron and batter to the table.

Serve your syrup warm and any berry toppings at room temperature. Sprinkle sliced strawberries or mixed raspberries and blackberries with a little sugar to get their juices running half an hour before your meal.

Lunch

Whether you are glued to sports on the tube, or surrounded by sections of the Sunday *Times*, any of these Sunday lunches would make a perfect, quiet companion.

All of the sandwiches are dripless and the salads are one-forkers. So, if you and yours are weekend vagabonds, you can mix and match your favorites and take the show on the road.

The burgers can all go outside to the grill for patio parties in the hot summer months.

Tony Soprano Steak Sandwiches with Giardiniera Relish

Feeds 4 people or 2 gangsters.

My salute to the greatest on-screen gangster since Don Corleone. I just love the big-hearted, murderous bastard and I know he'd love my sandwich. Salute and cent-an', Tony!

2 pounds of sirloin steak, 1 inch thick, trimmed of fat and connective tissue and cut into 2 pieces
2 tablespoons balsamic vinegar (2 splashes)
Montreal Steak Seasoning (by McCormick) or coarse salt and black pepper, to taste
1-quart jar giardiniera salad (pickled vegetables and peppers), found in Italian aisle
A handful fresh flat-leaf parsley
Juice of 1/2 lemon
Drizzle extra-virgin olive oil
1 loaf garlic bread, homemade or prepared, split in half lengthwise
Drizzle extra-virgin olive oil for pan
4 leaves romaine from the heart of the lettuce head

Pat trimmed steaks with paper towels and place on a plate. Rub each steak with a splash of balsamic vinegar and a sprinkle of steak seasoning or coarse salt and black pepper. Let meat rest.

Drain giardiniera salad and reserve juice. Place salad in a food processor with parsley, the lemon juice, and a drizzle of extra-virgin oil. Pulse-grind the mixture into a finely chopped relish.

Brown garlic bread loaf under broiler and remove from oven.

Wipe a drop of olive oil across a nonstick skillet and heat over medium-high heat till pan smokes. Add steaks to hot pan and cook 5 minutes on each side. Douse the pan with a few tablespoons of the juice from the pickled relish. Rub the steaks around, picking up the color and juice from the pan. Place steaks on a big cutting board and let rest for 10 minutes, allowing juices to distribute.

Slice steaks very thin, on an angle and against the grain. Pile meat on plate and scrape juice off board over the top of meat. Wipe off board.

Place garlic bread on board and cover bottom half with your relish. Rest piles of meat on top of relish. Top with leaves of romaine and the other half of garlic bread. Prick bread with long toothpicks and hack up super sub into four big hunks.

Just when you think life couldn't get any better, open up a sack of Terra brand Yukon Gold garlic and herb chips to munch along with your sandwich. Now life is really good.

Balsamic Chicken Sandwiches with Orange and Oregano Relish

Makes 4 sandwich rolls.

You will lose your mind over these! Don't operate heavy machinery after eating.

4 pieces boneless, skinless chicken breasts (2 full breasts total)
2 tablespoons balsamic vinegar (2 splashes)
Montreal Steak Seasoning (by McCormick) or coarse salt and black pepper, to taste
Extra-virgin olive oil
2 tablespoons water (a splash or two)

ORANGE AND OREGANO RELISH
5 navel oranges
3 sprigs fresh oregano, leaves stripped from stem and finely chopped (about 2 tablespoons)
1/2 small red onion, finely chopped
A drizzle extra-virgin olive oil
A splash red wine vinegar
A pinch salt and a couple grinds pepper

4 crusty sandwich rolls (cornmeal, sesame, or plain), split
4 leaves fresh Bibb, Boston, or red leaf lettuce

Rinse and dry chicken breasts with paper towels. Place on a dish and rub with a couple of splashes vinegar and seasoning. Drizzle olive oil on a nonstick griddle or skillet and heat over medium-high heat. Add chicken to pan; cook 5 minutes on the first side, a little less on the second. Add a splash of water to the pan and rub the chicken breasts around pan to pick up all the color and flavor. When water has evaporated, remove pan from heat. Let chicken rest before slicing.

While chicken is cooking, cut oranges into 6 wedges and use a paring knife to separate flesh from skins. Chop orange flesh and mix in a small bowl with oregano, red onion, oil and vinegar, and salt and pepper.

Slice chicken on an angle. Pile a sliced breast onto bottoms of rolls. Top with relish, lettuce, and tops of rolls.

This sandwich is good warm, at room temperature, or cold; at home, on the road, or in another state of being.

Chicken Caprese Club Rolls

Makes 4 sandwich rolls.

4 slices pancetta or center-cut bacon or peppered bacon
4 halves boneless, skinless chicken breasts
2 splashes balsamic vinegar
A couple grinds fresh pepper and a pinch salt
Extra-virgin olive oil
A splash water (1 to 2 tablespoons)
4 sesame sub rolls, split and crusted in warm oven
2 vine-ripened tomatoes or 4 firm plum tomatoes
$1/2$ pound smoked fresh mozzarella (in specialty cheese case of market), cut into thin slices
12 leaves fresh basil
A drizzle extra-virgin olive oil, for topping
Another pinch salt and pepper

Brown pancetta or bacon slices in a skillet over medium to medium-high heat, then place on paper towel–lined plate to drain.

Rub rinsed and dried chicken breasts with balsamic vinegar and pepper and salt. Wipe a grill pan or nonstick skillet with a touch of oil and cook breasts over medium-high heat 5 minutes on the first side, a minute less on the second. Add a splash of water and pick up all the color from the pan by rubbing breasts around in it. Remove from heat and allow juices to distribute.

Line up bottoms of subs across cutting board. Slice breasts on an angle into strips and pile chicken on each sandwich. Top with 2 slices cooked pancetta or bacon. Layer tomato and cheese slices across sandwich. Pile basil leaves one atop the other. Roll leaves into a log and slice very thin. Sprinkle an even amount of basil confetti over each sandwich. Drizzle with olive oil, salt, and pepper. Cap sandwiches with roll tops and split across the middle. Serve warm or at room temperature.

Wash it down with a little red wine. It's Sunday, you can enjoy some with your lunch. Pure bliss, and then an après-meal nap.

Another Antipasto Pie

Feeds up to 8.

Beyond being a terrific Sunday snack-all-afternoon sandwich, this completely self-contained, portable antipasto party makes a fantastic offering for a block party, a PTA function, an office party, or a tailgate gathering.

1 large, round loaf crusty bread, 10 to 12 inches across (If your bakery or market does not carry this daily, ask at the counter for one to be made up for you.)

GARBANZO BEAN SPREAD
1 can (15 ounces) garbanzo beans, rinsed and drained very well
2 sprigs fresh rosemary, leaves stripped from stem
A drizzle extra-virgin olive oil
2 small cloves garlic, coarsely chopped
Pinch salt and a grind black pepper

RELISH
One 16-ounce jar giardiniera relish
Juice of 1/2 lemon
A handful fresh flat-leaf parsley

1/4 pound pitted green and oil-cured or Kalamata black olives (from bulk olive section near deli counter)
1/2 pound slicing provolone
1/4 pound diced pepperoni or Abruzzese sausage
1/4 pound diced Genoa salami or sweet sopressata
2 roasted red bell peppers, home made or drained from jar
1 sack (10 ounces) mixed baby greens (from packaged salads section of produce department)
12 to 15 leaves fresh basil
A drizzle extra-virgin olive oil for dressing greens
A splash balsamic vinegar
Sweet or hot cherry peppers, to garnish

Cut top off bread and scoop out the guts.

Dump beans, rosemary, olive oil, garlic, and salt and pepper in food processor. Process till fairly smooth paste forms. Remove from processor. Rinse and dry processor bowl.

Put drained, pickled vegetable relish, lemon, parsley, and olives into processor and chop into a coarse relish. Remove mixture to bowl and rinse out processor.

Cover bottom of bread cavity with half of the provolone cheese. Spread the garbanzo bean dip on top with a plastic spatula. Add the relish in an even layer on top of that. Sprinkle on chopped meats. Top with the rest of the provolone cheese. Press the fillings down to make room for more. Top cheese with roasted peppers. Top peppers with a layer of mixed greens. Tear basil leaves and scatter onto greens. Drizzle with olive oil and a splash of balsamic vinegar. Place the top on the bread and stab with 8 long bamboo skewer picks every few inches to hold wedges in place while cutting them. Top skewers with sweet or hot cherry peppers for color and leave whole until ready to serve.

You will need your biggest, sharpest knife to cut this baby. Cut pie in the same order as you would a pizza—all the way across the middle, turn a quarter turn, cut all the way across again, then cut each quarter wedge in half, resulting in 8 even, mouth-stretching sandwiches.

Anywhere, anyplace you serve this dish, people will ooh and ah and ask you where you ever came up with such an idea. Answer with silence and a smile.

VARIATION:

For a vegetarian Antipasto Pie, simply omit the meats. To reduce fat and increase protein, use half the amount of cheese and add tuna in water, drained and chunked.

Butter Bean Salad

Makes 1 quart. Serves 4 to 6.

2 cans (15 ounces each) butter
   beans, rinsed and drained well
1/2 each red and green bell pepper,
   seeded and diced
1/2 small red onion, chopped
A handful fresh flat-leaf parsley,
   chopped

DRESSING
Juice of 1 large or 2 small lemons
3 tablespoons extra-virgin olive oil
   (3 times around the bowl)
2 cloves garlic, minced
1/2 teaspoon ground cumin
   (3 or 4 pinches)
Coarse salt and freshly ground
   pepper, to taste

Mix beans, peppers, onion, and parsley. Whisk dressing ingredients together and pour over salad. Toss well and serve.

Green Salad

Makes 4 side servings.

DRESSING
1/2 small white onion, grated over
   bowl with hand grater
1 tablespoon balsamic vinegar
   (a good splash)
3 tablespoons extra-virgin olive oil
   (3 times around the bowl)

A pinch sugar
Coarse salt and black pepper,
   to taste

1 sack (10 ounces) mixed baby
   greens

Whisk dressing ingredients together and toss over greens. Serve. Too simple?

Potato-No-Mayo Salad

Serves 6 to 8.

18 small red potatoes
6 baby carrots (from bulk bin in produce section), finely chopped
12 blades fresh chives, chopped
4 sprigs fresh tarragon, chopped (about 2 tablespoons)
1/2 small red onion, finely chopped

DRESSING
4 tablespoons extra-virgin olive oil (5 times around the bowl)
2 tablespoons white wine vinegar
1/2 small onion, grated into bowl with handheld grater
2 pinches sugar

Salt and pepper, to taste

Boil potatoes in deep pot of salted water till tender. Drain and cool the potatoes and quarter them. Combine dressing with whisk or fork and toss potatoes with finely chopped baby carrots, chives, tarragon, and red onion. Salt and pepper to taste. Serve at room temperature or chilled.

Fall and Winter Soup Lunch: Tortellini en Brodo

Serves up to 4.

1 sack (10 ounces) triple-washed fresh spinach
2 quarts (five 15-ounce cans) no-fat, low-sodium chicken broth

1 pound fresh cheese tortellini
2 pinches ground nutmeg
A couple grinds black pepper
Grated Parmigiano or Romano cheese

Remove large stems from spinach and coarsely chop leaves. Set aside.

Bring broth to a boil. Add tortellini and let broth return to a boil. Reduce heat and let simmer for 10 minutes. Add spinach and stir into soup until wilted. Add nutmeg and pepper and serve with lots of grated cheese and warm, crusty bread.

VARIATION:

Supper-up Your Soup

Add 1 pound bulk Italian sweet sausage, browned and drained, to your soup and turn it into a hearty country supper.

Spring and Summer Soup Lunch: Macho Gazpacho

Feeds up to 4.

1 large green bell pepper, seeded and cut into chunks

1 medium red onion, peeled and cut into chunks

1/2 European seedless cucumber, peeled and chunked

1 can (28 ounces) whole plum tomatoes, drained and seeded

1 can (48 ounces) tomato juice

8 shakes cayenne pepper sauce, Tabasco sauce, or Red Hot sauce

Coarse salt and black pepper, to taste

A palmful fresh cilantro leaves

2 cloves garlic, peeled and chopped

2 drizzles extra-virgin olive oil

4 green onions, thinly sliced

In food processor, add half of everything except the green onions—raw vegetables and canned tomatoes, tomato juice, cayenne, salt, pepper, cilantro, garlic, and a drizzle of extra-virgin olive oil. Pulse until soup is combined and fairly smooth. Pour into serving bowl or large pitcher. Repeat process with second batch. Serve in chilled mugs or bowls with a garnish of green onions and bread cubes or croutons. If you like it chunky, chop up a little extra cucumber, onion, and bell pepper to sprinkle on top.

• Pack gazpacho in a thermos and put paper cups in your knapsack and gazpacho goes to work or on a weekend road trip.

• Keep a few mugs in the freezer during the hot summer months to serve your Macho Gazpacho in.

• Supper up your soup with jumbo cooked, cleaned, and deveined shrimp for dipping in your Macho Gazpacho.

Better Burgers

The American All-Star Burger

Makes 5 burger patties.

BURGERS
1 1/2 pounds lean ground beef
1 small onion, minced
2 rounded tablespoons sweet pickle
   relish
4 drops cayenne pepper sauce
Montreal Steak Seasoning (by
   McCormick) or coarse salt and
   black pepper, to taste

BASTING SAUCE
Ketchup and steak sauce, 1/3
   cup each, mixed

TOPPINGS
Lettuce, tomato, red onion

5 crusty hard rolls, split

Mix burger ingredients and form into five patties. Cook patties on a nonstick griddle or in a nonstick skillet over medium-high heat for 5 minutes on one side, 4 on the other, basting with sauce after the flip. Pile patties on rolls and top as you like.

The Italian American: Beef Burgers with Old Country Influences

Makes 5 burgers.

BURGERS
1¹/₂ pounds lean ground beef
1 small can tomato paste
1 small onion, minced
2 cloves garlic, minced
2 stems fresh oregano, pulled off
  stems and chopped
10 leaves fresh basil, piled, rolled
  into a log, and slivered
Coarse salt, to taste
2 shakes crushed red pepper flakes

TOPPINGS
4 long green Italian peppers
  (cubanelle)
1 tablespoon extra-virgin olive oil
  (once around the pan)
1 can (14 ounces) prepared pizza or
  tomato sauce
6 slices provolone cheese

5 big, crusty, fresh sesame-seeded
  hard rolls

Mix all the burger ingredients and form into five patties.

Cook burgers 5 minutes on one side, 4 on the flip side, over medium-high heat on a nonstick skillet or griddle pan.

While burgers cook, fry peppers in a little olive oil in a second skillet over medium-high heat until tender.

Warm pizza or tomato sauce in microwave or small saucepan.

Pile burgers with peppers and cheese while they are still on the pan. Turn off heat and cover pan with a loose aluminum foil tent to melt cheese.

Place burgers in buns and top with warm pizza or tomato sauce. *Abbundanza!*

Thai Turkey Burgers

Feeds 4.

WARM PINEAPPLE SALSA
1 fresh, ripe, cored pineapple
   (available in the produce section)
1 tablespoon sesame oil (once
   around the pan)
1/4 teaspoon crushed red pepper
   flakes (a shake or two)
1/2 small red pepper, seeded and
   chopped
1/4 red onion, finely chopped
2 tablespoons dark brown sugar
   (a palmful)
10 to 15 fresh basil leaves, cut into
   thin strips

1 1/3 pounds ground turkey breast
1 inch fresh gingerroot, grated, or 2
   pinches ground ginger
2 cloves garlic, minced
2 tablespoons dark soy sauce
   (a couple glugs)
2 teaspoons curry powder (a third of
   a palmful)
Coarse salt, to taste
2 green onions, finely chopped

4 cornmeal-topped rolls, split, or 4
   toasted sandwich-size English
   muffins
Bibb, Boston, or red leaf lettuce
   for topping

Drain pineapple and cut into pieces that will fit in food processor. Place in processor and process to a coarse, chunky mixture. Heat sesame oil and crushed red pepper flakes in a skillet over medium-high heat until oil smokes. Add pepper and onion and cook a minute or two. Add pineapple and heat through. Sprinkle with brown sugar and cook another minute or two. Remove from heat and toss in basil. Let the salsa hang out in the warm pan while you cook burgers.

Heat a nonstick skillet or griddle pan over medium-high heat. Mix turkey, ginger, garlic, soy sauce, curry powder, salt, and green onions. Form into 4 patties and cook 4 minutes on each side. Serve on rolls with lots of warm pineapple salsa, lettuce, and a few of your favorite chips alongside.

Curried Turkey Pockets

Feeds 4.

1¹/₃ pounds ground turkey breast
2 tablespoons curry powder
2 shakes Worcestershire sauce
2 cloves garlic, minced
¹/₄ medium onion, grated
Chopped fresh cilantro (a palmful)
Coarse salt, to taste
4 large flour tortillas

Mango chutney (see Notes)
¹/₄ pound mixed baby greens,
    prewashed (sold in bulk in the
    produce section)
Thinly sliced red onion
2 carrots, shredded
Terra Chips (see Notes)

Combine turkey with curry, Worcestershire, garlic, grated onion, cilantro and a little salt. Form into 4 patties. Grill over medium-high gas heat or charcoal for 5 to 6 minutes per side.

Blister tortillas for 30 seconds per side over high heat on outdoor grill or griddle pan.

To assemble, spread center of tortilla with chutney. Pile on some lettuce, red onion, and carrot, topping off with a turkey pattie. Fold the tortilla up and over on all 4 sides. Flip entire tortilla over and cut the package from corner to corner, making 2 pockets. Feeds 4, with chips.

Notes:

Mango chutney is found in the condiments section of the market. Major Grey's, Patak's, and London Pub are the common brand names I've found. Chutney is often served with curries and is a delicious topper for this burger.

Serve with funky chips from the natural foods aisle. Try Terra Chips—root vegetable multicolored seasoned chips. Terra Chips is a brand name as well as a product name. The Terra Chips selection includes garlic and herb or salt and vinegar Yukon Gold chips, spiced taro root chips, and spiced or barbecued sweet potato chips. All of the Terra Chips products are lower in saturated fats than potato chips.

Pot-Sticker Pockets

Makes up to 8 pockets.

These pork burger sandwich pockets taste like a giant Chinese dumpling.

1¹/₂ pounds ground pork
¹/₂ cup (a good handful) chopped
  water chestnuts
2 green onions, chopped
2 tablespoons soy sauce (several
  good shakes)
¹/₂ teaspoon ground ginger or 1
  inch fresh gingerroot, grated
2 cloves garlic, minced
A pinch crushed red pepper
¹/₂ orange, outer skin grated into bowl,
  orange juiced into meat mixture

Hoisin sauce (available on the Asian
  foods aisle of the market)

TOPPINGS
¹/₄ cup white vinegar
2 teaspoons honey
1 cucumber, peeled and seeded,
  thinly sliced
¹/₂ carrot, shredded
Bibb lettuce leaves, shredded

8 large flour tortillas

Combine pork and next 7 ingredients in a bowl. Form into patties and cook for 5 minutes on each side on grill pan or outdoor grill over medium-high heat or hot coals. As burgers cook, baste with hoisin sauce.

Make topping by mixing honey and vinegar and coating cucumbers and carrot in the dressing. Wash and dry one head bibb lettuce. Shred by thinly slicing.

To heat all 8 flour tortillas, wrap in a slightly damp paper towel, then in aluminum foil, and place packet in 325°F oven or on grill until burgers are done. To heat individually, get a big skillet or griddle really hot and blister each tortilla for 15 seconds on each side (no oil necessary).

To assemble, place a palmful of lettuce in center of tortilla. Top with a couple scoops of cucumber and carrot salad and one pork pattie. Wrap tortilla up and over on all 4 sides and flip entire square-shaped packet over. Cut in half from corner to corner, forming 2 pockets.

Tramezzini
"The Greatest Grilled Cheeses"

Each recipe makes 4 sandwiches.

In little wine bars and roadside grills all over Italy, you can delight in tramezzini. Little grilled cheese sandwiches cooked in a contraption that looks like a waffle iron, these barely filled bites are simply *the* best.

On some sunny Sunday afternoon, in spring, summer, or fall, make some tramezzini. Pour yourself a small glass of wine and kick off your shoes. Take the kitchen chair out the back door and wander barefoot to your perfect spot in the sun. Eat off your lap. Take a sip of wine. Close your eyes and get lost in time, space, and place.

In the winter, free your soul by sitting by the fire with a tray of tramezzini, a bottle of wine, soft music, and someone special.

FILLINGS

Apricot jam, 1 teaspoon per sandwich, spread on 1 side of bread only
4 ounces fontina cheese, thinly sliced
4 thin slices prosciutto di Parma

⁂

4 to 6 ounces smoked fresh mozzarella, thinly sliced
2 medium portobello mushroom caps, very thinly sliced and sautéed in 1 tablespoon extra-virgin olive oil with 2 stems rosemary, leaves stripped and chopped, and coarse salt and black pepper, to taste

⁂

4 ounces reconstituted drained sun-dried tomatoes, chopped, or 12 pitted black oil-cured olives, chopped
2 sprigs fresh thyme, leaves stripped from stem and chopped
4 ounces soft goat cheese or Robiola (a soft, fresh cheese) or shaved ricotta salata
Black pepper, to taste

⁂

4 ounces fresh mozzarella, thinly sliced
12 cracked green olives, coarsely chopped
A pinch crushed red pepper flakes

⁂

1 cup defrosted chopped spinach, squeezed dry
2 tablespoons capers, smashed with edge of knife
4 ounces provolone, thinly sliced and trimmed to fit bread
4 anchovies melted in 2 tablespoons extra-virgin olive oil (1 teaspoon of this spread on only 1 side of bread)
2 cloves garlic, minced
2 pinches crushed red pepper flakes
Black pepper and a pinch of nutmeg per sandwich

Divide fillings equally among the 4 sandwiches, spreading them in layers and working to the edges of the bread.

Grill these sandwiches on a dry, preheated griddle or grill pan over moderate heat for 4 or 5 minutes on each side. Make them all on firm-sliced white toasting bread trimmed of crusts. Completely construct sandwiches and press together firmly before grilling. After grilling, cut sandwiches from corner to corner, forming 2 little triangles.

Sunday Suppers

I-Waited-All-Week Spaghetti Dinner

This will feed as many as it needs to—it just seems to work out that way.

GRAMPA EMMANUEL'S EVERYTHING SAUCE

8 cloves garlic, crushed

4 tablespoons extra-virgin olive oil

1/2 teaspoon crushed red pepper flakes (a few good pinches)

2 medium onions, chopped

1 cup dry red wine

4 cans (28 ounces each) crushed tomatoes

20 leaves fresh basil

1 cup no-fat, low-sodium chicken broth

1 cup no-fat, low-sodium beef broth

8 Italian sausages, 4 hot and 4 sweet

4 tablespoons, total, extra-virgin olive oil

4 boneless, skinless chicken breasts

4 boneless, skinless chicken thighs

1 1/2 pounds country-style pork spareribs, well trimmed and boned

Salt and pepper (optional)

16 Meatballs (recipe follows)

MEATBALLS

1 1/2 pounds ground beef

1/2 pound ground pork

1/2 cup milk (3 or 4 splashes)

2 large eggs, beaten

1 1/2 cups (3 good handfuls) Italian bread crumbs

1 bunch fresh flat-leaf parsley, chopped (1 cup)

1/2 cup grated Parmigiano or Romano cheese

3 cloves garlic, minced

1 medium onion, finely chopped

2 pounds spaghetti, or any other kind of pasta you like, cooked until al dente when you are ready to eat

Preheat oven to 375°F. Mix meatball ingredients together and form into 16 meatballs. Place on a lightly greased cookie sheet and roast 12 to 15 minutes, or until evenly browned. Remove from oven and set aside.

Take a large skillet, for browning meat, and the biggest, deepest pot you have or can beg or borrow, and place on stovetop. Put on some quiet music and comfortable slippers. You are gonna be here for a while, but it's worth it and everyone who eats this will love you for the effort.

Cook garlic in olive oil with crushed red pepper in the really big pot over medium heat till the garlic speaks by sizzling in the oil. Add onions and cook 10 minutes, or till soft. Add wine and cook 5 minutes. Add tomatoes, basil, and broth and bring to a bubble. Reduce heat to medium-low and let simmer.

Brown the sausages in some olive oil (once around the pan) in the big skillet over medium-high heat. Do not cook through, just brown the casings and remove sausage to paper–towel lined plate. Remove excess grease from pan and brown chicken breasts for 3 minutes or so on each side. Remove chicken breasts to a platter and brown chicken thighs. Add a touch of olive oil to the pan as you need it. Remove thighs to a platter and add pork spareribs. Brown pork spareribs on all sides, then remove from pan. Put meat pan in sink and let soak. Take a break. Have something to drink.

Sprinkle browned meats, except sausage, with a little salt and pepper, if you wish. If you watch your salt intake and do not want a spicy sauce, do not season meats.

Gently place the ribs in the sauce pot. Cover and cook 15 minutes, stirring occasionally.

Add chicken, sausage, and meatballs. Cook 15 minutes, uncovered, stirring gently with a wooden spoon.

Cover and cook 30 minutes over moderately low heat, stirring occasionally.

Sauce can be held on warm stove as long as needed.

When it's about time to eat, have the kids help in making a big tossed salad. Dress salad with just a simple oil and balsamic dressing and salt and pepper. Heat garlic bread or loaves of Italian semolina bread to get them nice and crusty. Place a big bowl of grated cheese on each end of the table.

To serve, carefully remove the meats to a serving platter, grouping like meats together as you go so everyone can have whatever combination they prefer.

Toss spaghetti with a little sauce to keep it from sticking and ladle more on top of each bowlful as you serve it.

Chicken in the Oven

Feeds 8 to 10.

Every person I know with an Italian woman in their family tree—mamma, zia or nona—remembers this dish from childhood as being their favorite. Chicken, potatoes, rosemary: simple food that has filled the stomachs and fed the souls of countless children for generations.

Extra-virgin olive oil	4 chickens, each about 2¹/₂ to 3
24 small white or red potatoes	pounds, split into 8 halves by
Coarse salt and pepper, to taste	butcher
1 bunch (8 to 10 sprigs) rosemary,	Coarse salt and black pepper, to
leaves stripped from stem and	taste
finely chopped	
8 jarred, pickled hot cherry peppers,	1 cup juice from jarred, pickled hot
thinly sliced	cherry peppers
16 cloves garlic, crushed and	
popped from skin	

Preheat oven to 350° F.

Coat the bottom of two roasting pans with olive oil. Cut potatoes into wedges and add to pans in single layers. Drizzle potatoes with enough oil to coat them, then season with salt and pepper and a little chopped rosemary. Sprinkle peppers and half of the garlic (8 cloves) on top of the potatoes.

Rinse and pat chickens dry. Make a paste on your cutting board by mincing the remaining garlic with rosemary, salt, and pepper. Rub the paste all over the chickens, top and bottom. Place birds, skin side up, into pans on top of the potatoes. Cover pans and place in hot oven.

Roast, basting occasionally with pan juices, until meat thermometer in chicken reads 165° F, or until juices run completely clear when skin is pricked at thickest part of thigh and potatoes are tender. Roasting time will be about 1 hour. Remove pans from oven and turn oven up to 400° F. Uncover and drizzle pepper juice over chicken. Return to oven to darken and crisp chicken skin, about 12 to 15 minutes.

Serve with a big tossed salad and lots of crusty bread.

VARIATION:

Hot peppers may be omitted. Use 1 cup of white wine, rather than pepper juice, to deglaze pan.

Cioppino: A Fine Kettle of Fish

Feeds up to 8.

SAUCE

1/3 cup extra-virgin olive oil (4 or 5
 times around the pan)
8 cloves garlic, crushed and minced
1/2 teaspoon crushed red pepper
 flakes (a few good pinches)
2 stalks celery, from the heart, finely
 chopped
1 medium onion, finely diced
1 1/2 cups dry white wine (3 or 4
 good glugs)
1 cup no-fat, low-sodium chicken
 broth, or clam juice if you like a
 stronger fish flavor
2 cans (28 ounces each) crushed
 tomatoes
1 bay leaf
4 sprigs fresh thyme, leaves stripped
 from stem (about 1 tablespoon),
 chopped
A palmful fresh flat-leaf parsley,
 chopped

SEAFOOD

1/2 pound calamari (squid), skinned,
 cleaned, and cut into small pieces
1 pound cod, cut into 3-inch chunks
Salt and pepper, to taste
12 to 16 large shrimp, deveined
 and peeled
1 pound sea scallops (12 to 16
 pieces)
12 clams, well scrubbed
12 mussels, well scrubbed

1 loaf garlic bread, storebought or
 homemade, cut into chunks when
 you are ready to serve

In a very big kettle, heat oil, garlic, and crushed red pepper over medium heat. Add celery and onion and cook for 5 minutes to soften and mellow vegetables. Add white wine and allow wine to reduce by half, another 5 minutes or so. Add chicken broth or clam juice, tomatoes, bay, thyme, and parsley. Bring to a bubble and lower heat to a simmer.

Add squid to pot and cook 3 to 5 minutes. Next, set the cod in sauce and cook 7 or 8 minutes, giving the pot a shake now and then—do not stir with a spoon or you will break up the fish. Season with salt and pepper, adjusting to your taste.

Add shrimp, scallops, clams, and mussels and cover pot. Cook a last 5 to 8 minutes or until clams and mussels open. Gently give the kettle a shake or two to coat seafood in sauce. Scoop out into big, shallow bowls and serve with big chunks of garlic bread. Slurping, shucking with your hands, and licking your fingertips is proper etiquette for this dish. If you do not like such behavior at your dinner table, don't serve this.

Splendid Sing-a-Long Paella

Feeds 8.

So much fun, you'll need to break into song.

4 tablespoons extra-virgin olive oil (4 times around the pan)

6 cloves garlic, chopped

1/2 teaspoon crushed red pepper flakes (a couple pinches)

3 boneless, skinless chicken breasts, cut into chunks

3 boneless, skinless chicken thighs, cut into chunks

3/4 pound chorizo, chourico, or linguica, sliced on an angle 3/4 inch thick

1 large Spanish onion, chopped

1 red bell pepper, seeded and diced

3 cups enriched white rice, rinsed

1/2 teaspoon saffron threads (a few good pinches broken threads)

1 bay leaf, fresh or dried

3 cups no-fat, low-sodium chicken broth

3 cups boiling water

6 sprigs fresh thyme, leaves stripped from stem (about 2 tablespoons) and chopped

Coarse salt and black pepper, to taste

1 pound large shrimp, peeled and deveined

Eight 3-ounce lobster tails, shells split down underbelly with kitchen scissors

1 pound large shrimp, peeled and deveined

16 mussels, scrubbed

16 clams, scrubbed

1 cup defrosted frozen peas

Zest of 2 lemons

1/4 cup chopped pimientos, drained and diced

A handful capers, smashed with flat of knife

A handful chopped fresh flat-leaf parsley

Lemon wedges

Hunks of crusty bread

Chopped green onions, for garnish

In a large, deep skillet or a paella pan, heat oil, garlic, and crushed pepper over medium to medium-high heat. When garlic speaks by sizzling in oil, add chicken and brown. Add chorizo, onion, and bell pepper and sauté 5 minutes, giving the pan a shake now and again. Add rice and saffron and cook 5 minutes. Add bay leaf, broth, water, thyme, and salt and pepper. Cover with lid or tightly wrapped aluminum foil and reduce heat to a simmer. Cook 20 minutes, stirring occasionally. Add lobster and shrimp. Cover and cook 3 minutes. Add mussels and clams. Cover and cook till shells open. Remove cover and sprinkle pan with peas, lemon zest, pimiento, capers, and parsley. Give the pan a couple of shakes to loosely combine.

Surround edges of pan with lemon wedges, hunks of crusty bread or garlic bread, and a sprinkle of sliced green onions.

Enjoy!

Beef Barolo

Feeds 8.

Like beef burgundy, but my Mamma likes Barolo wine better.

1/4 **pound pancetta or center-cut bacon, chopped**
2 **carrots, peeled and finely diced**
2 **medium onions, finely diced**
2 **stalks celery from heart, finely diced**
8 **button or crimini mushroom caps, chopped**

4 **tablespoons extra-virgin olive oil**
4 **cloves garlic, crushed**
4 **pounds top sirloin roast, trimmed and cut into chunks**
4 **tablespoons all-purpose flour (a couple handfuls)**
Coarse salt and black pepper, to taste

1 **bottle Italian Barolo red wine or Spanish Rioja, less half a glass for the cook**
3 to 4 **tablespoons tomato paste**
1 **can (15 ounces) no-fat, low-sodium chicken broth**
2 **bay leaves, fresh or dried**
6 **sprigs fresh thyme, leaves stripped from stem, about 2 tablespoons, chopped**
4 **sprigs rosemary, stripped from stem and finely chopped**
A handful chopped fresh flat-leaf parsley

In a small skillet, cook pancetta or bacon over medium-high heat. When pancetta or bacon is lightly browned, add veggies to skillet and cook, stirring frequently, until veggies are tender, 3 to 5 minutes. Remove from heat and set aside.

In a big, deep pot, heat half the oil and garlic and brown half the meat over medium-high flame. When meat is brown, add a sprinkle of flour, salt, and pepper and cook another minute or two. Remove from pan and repeat process with second batch. When the second batch is done, add the first batch of meat back to pot and pour in the wine. Stir in tomato paste until it is dissolved in the wine. Pour in broth, and add just enough water to cover meat. Add bay leaves and sprinkle with thyme, rosemary, and parsley.

Bring to a boil, reduce heat to a simmer, cover, and cook 1 hour. After an hour, check meat to see if it is tender. If the meat is still a little tough, continue to cook, checking every 15 minutes for desired degree of doneness.

Serve with a tossed salad and your choice of steamed potatoes, buttered egg noodles, egg fettuccine with chive butter, or just a lot of warm, crusty bread for dipping.

Mixed Grill

For families like my own who can never agree on what to have for dinner, this mix of a little of this and a little of that seems to hush everyone up.

BEEF
2 pounds top sirloin, 1 to 1¼ inches thick, trimmed and cut into 8 boneless small steaks (Bring meat to room temperature before cooking—30 minutes, covered, on countertop.)
1 tablespoon extra-virgin olive oil (once around the pan), to coat
6 cloves garlic, crushed
2 to 3 tablespoons sherry (2 times around pan in steady stream) to deglaze

PORK
8 thin-cut boneless pork loin chops, 1½ to 2 pounds

MARINADE
3 tablespoons low-sodium soy sauce (a few good splashes)
2 tablespoons extra-virgin olive oil (twice around the bowl)
¼ teaspoon ground ginger
1 tablespoon sherry (a splash)
1 tablespoon balsamic vinegar (a splash)

Mix together ingredients for marinade and set chops in it. Let stand for 30 minutes at room temperature, covered with plastic wrap.

Reserve marinade for deglazing pan (removing pan-drippings with liquid).

CHICKEN
16 to 20 chicken tenders, 1½ to 2 pounds

MARINADE
3 tablespoons low-sodium soy sauce (a few splashes)

2 tablespoons extra-virgin olive oil (twice around the bowl)
¼ teaspoon ground ginger
1 tablespoon sherry (a splash)
1 tablespoon balsamic vinegar (a splash)
1 teaspoon honey (a drizzle)

Mix together ingredients for marinade. Set chicken in marinade, cover with plastic wrap, and let stand for 30 minutes at room temperature. Reserve marinade for deglazing pan.

LAMB
1½ pounds loin lamb chops (Have your butcher cut them very thin.)

MARINADE
Juice of 1 ripe lemon
1 tablespoon balsamic vinegar (a splash)
2 tablespoons extra-virgin olive oil
2 cloves garlic, minced

Mix together ingredients for marinade and put lamb in it. Set out for 30 minutes, as per others. Reserve juice to deglaze pan.

Mixed Grill Method: Cooking in tandem is important. Enlist the help of a second set of hands. Every meat is cooked using the same method. Place a touch of oil (once around the pan) into 2 nonstick skillets placed on the front 2 burners of stovetop over medium-high heat. When oil smokes, take 2 platters of meat, 1 variety for each pan, and add meat in single layer; cook 2 to 3 minutes on each side. For the beef, cook garlic cloves alongside. Pile meat up, each kind on a separate dish. Deglaze the pan with sherry or marinade and pour juices down over the top of each meat. Wipe out pans and return to stove to finish cooking all the meats.

Serve all the meats and accompaniments right from the stovetop and kitchen counters, making an impromptu buffet, or transfer items to dishes and line them up down the center of the dinner table.

Side Dishes for Mixed Grill

Mushrooms

30 small, whole mushroom caps
1 tablespoon extra-virgin olive oil
  (once around pan)
1 tablespoon butter (as marked on
  stick)
8 cloves garlic, minced

$1/4$ cup sherry (a couple good
  splashes)
$1/2$ lemon
Coarse salt and black pepper, to
  taste
A handful fresh flat-leaf parsley,
  chopped

Brown mushrooms in olive oil and butter over medium-high heat. Add garlic and shake pan, cooking another minute. Douse pan with sherry. Reduce sherry by half, cooking another minute or two, shaking pan frequently. Squeeze juice of $1/2$ lemon over pan. Sprinkle with salt, pepper, and a handful of parsley. Turn off heat and let stand till ready to serve.

Potatoes and Onions

Preheat oven to 425°F.

Slice cleaned white potatoes, 1 per person, into wedges and drop into a big bowl. Halve peeled medium onions, 1 per person, and add to potatoes. Drizzle with just enough extra-virgin olive oil to coat and sprinkle with Montreal Steak Seasoning blend or salt and pepper to taste. Pour out onto a nonstick cookie sheet or two, if needed, to cook in a single layer. Roast for 20 minutes or until golden and tender, turning once at midway point.

Mixed Vegetables

2 heads broccoli, split into florets, or 4 bunches broccolini, stems removed

1/2 pound baby carrots
1 small zucchini, sliced
1/2 lemon, sliced

Place veggies in saucepan. Add enough water to just cover the bottom of the pan. Place a few slices of lemon on top of veggies. Cover pot and put on back burner of stove. When you are 10 minutes away from serving, bring water to a boil, reduce heat to low, and steam for 3 to 5 minutes, or until veggies reach desired doneness. Remove from heat and serve or toss with a touch of butter and a squeeze of lemon juice.

Timing Notes on Side Dishes

Begin roasting potatoes and onions when you begin marinating meats. Cook mushrooms just before placing meats in pans to cook. Leave mushrooms in pan, covered, on warm stovetop as you cook meats. Get vegetables ready to steam as you reach the midway point in cooking all the meats. Cover, and place on back burner of stove but don't steam until meats are almost done.

Sunday Lasagna

Feeds 8.

MARINARA SAUCE
2 tablespoons extra-virgin olive oil
6 cloves garlic, minced
2 pinches crushed red pepper
3/4 pound lean ground beef
    (optional)
1 medium onion, minced
2 cans (28 ounces each) crushed
    tomatoes
A few leaves fresh basil, shredded
2 sprigs fresh oregano, stems
    stripped and oregano chopped
    (about 1 tablespoon)
A pinch salt

FILLING
Mix:
2 pounds part-skim ricotta
A pinch ground nutmeg
Salt and pepper, to taste
A palmful fresh flat-leaf parsley,
    chopped
1/2 pound provolone cheese, diced
    in small cubes

1 pound fresh (not dried) lasagna
    noodles or egg lasagna noodles,
    no frills on edges
1 cup grated Parmigiano cheese
1 pound fresh mozzarella, sliced

Preheat oven to 375°F.

For marinara sauce, heat olive oil and garlic and crushed red pepper in a deep pot over medium heat till garlic speaks by sizzling in oil. If making a meat sauce, add meat and onion to pan (if you would like plain lasagna, add just minced onion). Cook meat and/or onion for 10 minutes, until onion is very soft and sweet. Add tomatoes, basil, oregano, and salt. Bring to a bubble, reduce heat, and let simmer 10 minutes.

While sauce is simmering, combine ingredients for filling.

Line a lasagna pan with a couple of ladles of sauce, about 1/2 cup. Place a layer of lasagna noodles on top of sauce. Cover with a layer of cheese filling. Add a touch of grated cheese and a few dots of sauce. Place another layer of noodles in pan going in opposite direction, breaking pasta if need be to make it fit. Repeat process till pan is full. Top with mozzarella cheese.

Cover pan with plastic wrap, then aluminum foil. Place in oven and cook 45 minutes to 1 hour, or until liquid is absorbed and noodles are tender. Uncover and place under broiler to brown cheese. Serve with a big tossed salad.

Home for the Holidays

Soothing Comfort Foods

When Less is More

When preparing a holiday meal, keep in mind that you deserve a holiday, too. This section can help make holiday meals painless—for your back, legs, and feet! Begin with being reasonable. We do not need to gain ten pounds in three days. We all make far too much food for every holiday table and the happy family soon turns on you when eating leftovers for the fifth night. Keep it simple. Pick a starter, an entrée, three side dishes, and that's it. Eight to twelve happy faces, including yours.

Premeal, place small trays of cheeses, grapes, pears, and smoked almonds strategically throughout the house.

For an elegant transition between starter and meal, offer palate-cleansing small dishes of lemon sorbet with slivered fresh mint.

For desserts, check out the no-bake section that follows later on page 21. Mix in pies, cakes, and bouche de Noel from the professionals. Swallow your pride and show off your baking acumen during a less hectic time.

Making cookies with the kids is an exception. Never omit any tradition guarded by the children. They are the ones who hold holidays most dear. Children remember what many of us have forgotten, that holidays are really about grateful togetherness, family, happiness.

**Each of the recipes in this section feeds from 8 to 12
unless otherwise noted.**

Starters

Emmanuel's Stuffed Artichokes

One large artichoke will feed 3 or 4 as an appetizer, but allow 1 per person for a meal. This recipe calls for 3 large or 4 medium artichokes to serve 12 people.

3 large or 4 medium artichokes

Juice of 1 lemon, to boil artichokes with

$^1/_2$ cup extra-virgin olive oil

12 to 16 anchovies (You won't taste them later; use even if you don't like them.)

12 cloves garlic, minced

3 to $3^1/_2$ cups Italian bread crumbs

Freshly ground black pepper, to taste

1 cup grated Parmigiano Reggiano cheese

1 cup fresh flat-leaf parsley, chopped

Trim off stem of artichokes and, with a pair of kitchen scissors, trim tips of outer leaves down so the edges are even. Boil artichokes for 12 to 15 minutes in salted water with added lemon juice. Drain upside down on paper towels for several minutes, until cool enough to handle. Trim out the top of the heart of the artichoke (the choke itself). To do this, gently separate the leaves at the center, using a spoon, then scoop from the edge of the choke in and around to the other side and remove the spiny fibers.

Preheat oven to 450°F.

While artichoke cooks in water, heat oil over medium heat in your biggest skillet. Add anchovies and garlic and cook until anchovies melt into the oil. Add bread crumbs, 2 cups at first, then a little more at a time until oil is absorbed. You want the crumbs to remain loose, not damp and stuck together; add enough bread crumbs to achieve this texture. Toast until crumbs are evenly golden brown, about 5 minutes. Sprinkle in black pepper, cheese, and parsley. Place an artichoke in a shallow baking dish. Stuff a little stuffing at the base of each leaf, working in a circular pattern, into the center of the choke. Mound up any extra stuffing in the middle.

Drizzle dish with a touch of extra olive oil and heat in oven 5 to 10 minutes to crisp stuffing and edges of leaves. Serve hot with extra plate for the discarded leaves.

Rosie's Caramelized Onion Risotto

Feeds 8 to 12.

Rosie ordered the most divine risotto at lunch one day. I hope this comes close for both our sakes, because the restaurant we were dining at was out of town. Kudos to our friend David as well—he chose the restaurant.

2 tablespoons extra-virgin olive oil
4 large onions, thinly sliced
1 teaspoon sugar
Salt and pepper, to taste
7 cups chicken broth
2 cloves garlic, cracked and removed
    from skin
1 1/2 tablespoons extra-virgin olive oil

3 tablespoons butter
3 cups arborio rice
3/4 cup grated Parmigiano cheese
4 sprigs fresh thyme, leaves stripped
    from stem and chopped (2 table-
    spoons)
4 ounces pancetta or lean bacon,
    chopped and browned, for garnish

In a heavy-bottomed pot, heat oil over medium heat. Add onions and cook 15 minutes. Add sugar and cook until deep caramel brown in color, another 30 minutes. Stir frequently to keep sugars being released from onions from burning. Season onions with a little salt and pepper. Transfer half the onions at a time to food processor and grind into a smooth, thick paste. Scrape into mixing bowl with rubber spatula and let stand.

Heat broth in a medium pot over medium heat.

In a large, deep skillet or Dutch oven, heat garlic in olive oil and butter over medium heat. When garlic speaks by sizzling in oil, remove cloves from pan. Add arborio and coat well with butter and oil. Add a cup of hot stock and stir and cook until liquid is absorbed. Repeat until all of the broth is absorbed. It will take 2 or 3 minutes to incorporate each cup of liquid. Hand off stirring duty to as many family members as you can reach and drag into your place at the stove. Risotto should have a creamy, porridge-like consistency and the entire process should take about 20 minutes. Remove from stove and stir in onions, cheese, and thyme. Place on plates and serve immediately with a garnish of pancetta. It's a lot of work, but so worth it. Make up for it by choosing simpler recipes for the rest of the meal.

Holiday Stuffed Mushrooms

Feeds 8 to 12.

36 medium mushroom caps or 24
large stuffing mushrooms, 10
stems reserved
2 tablespoons extra-virgin olive oil

STUFFING
2 tablespoons extra-virgin olive oil
1 small onion, finely chopped
2 cloves garlic, minced
1 cup Italian bread crumbs (a couple
heaping handfuls)

2 ounces fontina, shredded ($1/4$ to
$1/3$ cup)
$1/4$ cup grated Parmigiano cheese
(a handful)
4 ounces chopped pancetta,
browned and drained
1 large egg, beaten

$1/4$ red bell pepper, finely diced, for
garnish

Preheat oven to 350°F.

Clean mushroom caps with damp paper towel. Heat olive oil in skillet over medium-high heat. Quickly sauté mushrooms until caps begin to become dark and tender and have rendered their juices. Remove from heat. Transfer mushrooms to small, flat baking pan, draining liquid from insides of caps as you remove from skillet. Wipe out skillet and return to heat.

Heat olive oil in skillet and sauté onion, garlic, and reserved mushroom stems, chopped. Sauté until tender and remove from heat. Combine mixture with remaining ingredients for stuffing in a medium bowl. Hold, covered, until ready to serve mushrooms.

Using a melon baller or a fingertip, mound stuffing onto caps. Bake 10 to 15 minutes, or until golden. Top each with a dot of chopped red bell pepper and serve, 3 per person for medium caps, 2 per person for large.

Real French Onion Soup with Gruyère Croutons

Feeds 8 to 12.

1 baguette, ends trimmed and sliced into 12 pieces, slicing on an angle
1/2 stick (4 tablespoons) butter
5 large onions, peeled, halved, and thinly sliced
1/2 teaspoon ground thyme (6 or 7 pinches)
8 cups beef broth

5 cups chicken broth
Salt and pepper, to taste
1/2 pint heavy (whipping) cream
2 cups grated Gruyère cheese
4 sprigs fresh thyme, leaves stripped from stem and chopped (2 tablespoons)

Lightly toast both sides of bread under broiler, then set aside.

Melt butter in a heavy-bottomed pot over medium heat. Add onions and thyme and cook until caramel brown in color, stirring frequently to prevent burning the sugars that are cooking out of the onions. Add broths and a little bit of salt and pepper. Bring to a boil, then reduce heat. Cover and cook soup 30 minutes. Turn off heat and let stand until ready to serve.

To serve, bring soup back up to a bubble over medium heat. Stir in cream. Ladle soup into heat-resistant crocks or small, deep bowls. Place bowls on cookie sheets. Top bowls with toast and a handful of grated cheese. Place a tray of bowls carefully under broiler until cheese is brown and bubbling. Sprinkle with thyme and slide bowls onto cool underliner to place on table. Do not give children under five a hot bowl. Serve little ones a cup of soup with a cheesy toast on the side.

Fresh Figs and Prosciutto

Feeds 8 to 12.

24 fresh figs, quartered
2 tablespoons extra-virgin olive oil
  (2 times around the bowl)

A splash balsamic vinegar
A pinch coarse salt and a grind pepper
12 slices prosciutto di Parma

Combine figs with oil and vinegar and salt and pepper. Toss and plate 8 pieces of fig per person. Arrange a ribbon of prosciutto across the plate of figs and serve.

Champagne Shrimp

Feeds 8 to 12.

36 large shrimp, peeled and
  deveined (Devein under running
  water and butterfly by splitting
  shrimp to, but not through, the
  underbelly of the shrimp.)
4 tablespoons butter
2 shallots, finely chopped
1/2 bottle brut (dry) champagne

Salt and pepper, to taste
1 half-pint heavy (whipping) cream
2 pinches ground white pepper or 2
  of cayenne
Zest of 2 lemons, for garnish
4 sprigs fresh tarragon, pulled off
  stems and chopped (2 tablespoons), for garnish

Pat shrimp dry. Melt butter in a large skillet over medium heat. Add shallots and sauté for a couple of minutes. Add champagne, salt, and pepper. Bring to a boil and reduce by half, 4 or 5 minutes. Add shrimp and cook 3 minutes, or until pink. Remove shrimp to plate with slotted spoon and cover loosely with aluminum foil tent. Reduce sauce by half again, another 5 minutes or so. Add cream and let sauce cook, stirring continuously, until it thickens. Add white or cayenne pepper and remove from heat. Place shrimp on serving plates and top with a little sauce and sprinkle with lemon zest and tarragon.

Italian Sea Salad

Feeds 8 to 12.

1 pound cleaned small squid (from
  frozen seafood section of market)
1 cup lemon juice (the juice of 8
  lemons)

DRESSING
1/2 cup extra-virgin olive oil (a few
  good glugs)
Salt and pepper, to taste
4 pinches crushed red pepper flakes
  (1/4 teaspoon)

2 pinches ground thyme (1/8 teaspoon)
3 cloves garlic, minced
A palmful fresh flat-leaf parsley
  (2 tablespoons), chopped

Two 8-ounce lobster tails, steamed,
  meat removed from shell and
  chopped
3/4 pound cooked crabmeat
10 large cooked shrimp, cut up

Cook squid in 1 quart of salted water with lemon juice added. Bring to a boil and
simmer 5 minutes. Drain and run under cold water to cool. Slice squid into rings.

Mix dressing ingredients with a whisk. Place lobster, crab, shrimp, and squid
in a bowl and toss with dressing.

Entrées

Roast Turkey with Apple and Onion Stuffing and Gravy

Feeds 8 to 12.

THE BIRD
One 14-pound turkey, cleaned very
   well and dried
Coarse salt and black pepper, to
   taste
1 medium onion, quartered
1 carrot, peeled and quartered

1 stalk of celery, quartered
1 clove garlic
2 bay leaves
1 stick (8 tablespoons) butter or
   margarine, softened
1 cup no-fat, low-sodium chicken
   broth

Season the bird inside and out with salt and pepper. Place the turkey in a roast-ing pan. Fill cavity with vegetables, garlic, and bay leaves. Place half the butter inside bird with vegetables and pour in 1/2 cup of broth. Place remaining broth in pan and slather bird with remaining butter. Nest a thermometer in thickest part of thigh. Cover pan with roaster lid or extra-wide aluminum foil.

When you are ready to roast, preheat oven to 300°F and roast bird 3 to 4 hours, until it registers 160°F on a meat thermometer. Take the aluminum foil or lid off turkey and ladle out the pan juices. Turn oven up to 500°F and brown skin for 7 or 8 minutes. Wow, are you good—what a bird! Remove bird to carving board and reserve any remaining juices, adding them to those ladled out earlier. Let stand 20 minutes before carving, or until you are good and ready for everyone to sit down.

GRAVY
Pan drippings, skimmed of fat, from
   above recipe
2 cans (15 ounces each) chicken broth

4 tablespoons all-purpose flour
Salt and pepper, to taste
1/2 teaspoon ground thyme (eyeballed in the palm of your hand)

In a big saucepan, heat drippings and broth over medium heat. Remove 1 ladle of broth, and mix flour into it until smooth. Pour into sauce and whisk until gravy thickens. Season with salt, pepper, and thyme.

STUFFING
1 stick (8 tablespoons) butter
2 medium onions, chopped
6 stalks celery, finely diced
4 medium Macintosh apples,
    washed but not peeled; cored
    and chopped

Salt and pepper, to taste
2 cups chicken broth
A handful fresh flat-leaf parsley,
    chopped (1/4 cup)
Half a palmful (1 tablespoon) poultry
    seasoning
8 cups seasoned stuffing mix

This can be made two days ahead and just thrown in the oven 45 minutes before the turkey comes out.

Melt butter in a large pan over medium heat. Sauté onions and celery until tender, 7 to 10 minutes. Add apples and cook another 3 or 4 minutes until tender. Season pan with salt and pepper to taste—go easy. Add broth, parsley, and poultry seasoning and bring to a bubble. Add stuffing and combine until liquid is absorbed. Grease a flat pan and form a rounded loaf out of stuffing mixture. Cover and refrigerate until ready to bake.

Bake at 350°F with turkey until crispy on top and warm though, 35 to 45 minutes. Loosen with long, skinny spatula and slide over to warm serving platter. Garnish with fresh whole cranberries nested in leafy kale along a small stretch of the platter's rim.

The Easiest Leftover Soup Ever: Stuffin' Soup

Serves up to 6.

Special bonus recipe, no extra charge.

Leftover stuffing, whatever you've
  got, warmed in 300°F oven
1 tablespoon olive oil
2 carrots, peeled and diced
1 yellow-skinned medium onion,
  chopped
2 stalks celery, chopped
3 pinches poultry seasoning
1 bay leaf

Coarse salt and black pepper, to
  taste
One 48-ounce plus two 15-ounce
  cans no-fat, low-sodium chicken
  broth
2 cups leftover turkey meat, pulled
  from bones and coarsely chopped
A handful fresh flat-leaf parsley,
  chopped

Heat olive oil in a deep pot over medium-high heat. Add vegetables, poultry seasoning, bay leaf, and a little salt and pepper. Reduce heat to medium and cover. Sweat the vegetables for 5 minutes, stirring occasionally. Add broth and turkey. Bring to a boil, reduce heat, and simmer 10 minutes. Remove stuffing from oven and, using an ice cream scoop, place a scoop of stuffing in each soup bowl. Ladle soup around stuffing and sprinkle with parsley. Spoon from stuffing as you eat through soup. Way-cool.

Baked Ham

Feeds 8 to 12

One 12 to 14-pound cured country-
  style ham, bone in (Smithfield or
  like variety)
1 gallon apple cider (optional)

BASTING MIXTURE
1/2 cup maple syrup
1 cup all-fruit apricot preserves
1/2 cup bourbon

Place ham in a large pot or bowl, cover with water, and refrigerate overnight.

Take ham out of water and trim excess fat. Put ham back in fresh water or cider to cover. Place pot on stove and bring to a boil. Reduce heat and let simmer for 4 hours. Remove from water. Place on rack in roasting pan. Combine all ingredients for Basting Mixture with a fork or a whisk. Brush ham with basting mixture. Place ham in preheated 350°F oven and roast, basting occasionally, for 30 minutes.

Roast Prime Rib of Beef au Jus with Popovers

Feeds 8 to 12.

One 9-pound boneless rib roast,
    trimmed by butcher of all the fat
1/2 cup Montreal Steak Seasoning
    (by McCormick) or coarse salt and
    black pepper, to taste

1 tablespoon all-purpose flour
1 cup beef broth
1/2 cup good dry red wine

Take roast out of fridge. Coat generously with seasoning or salt and pepper all over. Set roast out at room temperature for 3 hours, covered with plastic wrap.

Preheat oven to 400°F. Place beef on rack in roasting pan. Place pan in center of oven. Roast 20 minutes and reduce heat to 325°F. Continue to roast meat for a total of 18 minutes per pound for rare, 20 for medium, 22 for well done. For medium rare take meat out of oven when meat thermometer registers 125°F. Let meat rest 15 minutes on carving board. Skim fat from drippings. Whisk flour into drippings. Transfer to saucepan, add broth and wine, and bring to a boil. Reduce heat and simmer 5 minutes. Slice meat and top with jus.

Popovers

Yields 12 popovers.

3 tablespoons butter
3 large eggs
3 cups milk
3 cups all-purpose flour

1 1/2 teaspoons salt

12 custard cups or ramekins,
    greased well and placed on flat pan

Preheat oven to 375°F.

Melt butter in saucepan over low heat. Beat eggs in big bowl on low speed with electric hand mixer till frothy. Add milk and butter and beat until just blended. Add flour and salt and beat until the batter is smooth. Fill custard cups 3/4 full and bake 1 hour. Remove from oven and cut small slits in tops of popovers to release steam. Place back in oven and cook another 10 minutes. Remove from cups and serve hot.

If serving with a roast cooked at a different temperature, hold popovers, removed from their baking cups, on a metal pan in a warm place, uncovered, until your roast comes out of oven.

Roast Loin of Pork

Feeds 8 to 12.

One 6- to 7-pound pork loin, boned
but not tied and cleaned of all fat
6 tablespoons minced garlic
Zest of 1 lemon
2 tablespoons coarse salt
A handful fresh flat-leaf parsley
2 tablespoons (4 sprigs fresh,
minced) each thyme, rosemary,
and sage

2 tablespoons extra-virgin olive oil
Black pepper
1/2 cup Italian bread crumbs
1 cup dry white wine
4 cups chicken broth
4 tablespoons all-purpose flour

Preheat oven to 500°F.

Pat meat dry. Make a paste by chopping garlic, lemon zest, salt, and parsley together on your cutting board until finely minced. Combine in a small dish with thyme, rosemary, and sage until well mixed. Rub meat with olive oil. Cover with herb crust. Grind generous amount of black pepper over herb-covered roast. Spread bread crumbs across your cutting board. Roll herbed roast in them to coat evenly. Place pork in roasting pan, place pan on center rack in oven and cook for 15 minutes, then reduce heat to 350°F and cook 45 to 55 minutes, until it registers 160° on meat thermometer. Let meat rest on carving board. Skim fat from drippings and transfer drippings to saucepan. Add wine and broth. Heat to boiling, then reduce heat to medium-low. Mix flour into 1 ladleful of sauce, pour back into pot, and whisk until gravy thickens.

A Brisket Every Bubbe Will Love

Feeds 8 to 12.

You will need a very large and wide pot or you'll have to use two pots, dividing the recipe equally between the two pans.

Two 5-pound pieces brisket of beef
4 cloves garlic, coarsely chopped

Black pepper, to taste
2 bay leaves

MARINADE
1/2 cup extra-virgin olive oil
8 sprigs fresh thyme (about 3 to 4 tablespoons when chopped)
8 leaves fresh sage, chopped
1/4 cup red wine vinegar (a couple splashes)
Juice of 1 lemon
2 teaspoons kosher salt (half a palmful)

1/4 cup extra-virgin olive oil
1 large onion, chopped
8 cups chicken stock or broth
4 cups water
2 tablespoons soy sauce (a good splash)
Salt and pepper, to taste

Poke meat to make small incisions throughout and fill with bits of garlic. Mix remaining marinade ingredients together. Place briskets in a shallow dish and pour marinade over the top. Refrigerate overnight.

Heat oil in the bottom of your brisket pot(s) over medium-high heat. Brown onion, stirring frequently, and remove from pan. Remove meat from marinade and shake off excess. Reserve marinade. Place meat in hot pan and brown all over on high heat. Add broth, reserved marinade, water, soy sauce, salt, and pepper to the pan. Bring to a a boil, reduce heat, cover and simmer 2 1/2 hours, or until meat is easily pierced with a fork and is very tender.

> **For brisket vegetables, add 12 medium peeled potatoes, 6 quartered carrots, and 6 quartered celery stalks to broth for last 60 minutes of cooking time.**

Christmas Pasta

Feeds 8 to 12

2 tablespoons extra-virgin olive oil
(twice around the pan)
2 pounds sweet Italian sausage,
bulk or removed from casings
1 pound lean ground beef
1/2 pound pancetta, chopped

2 medium onions, finely chopped
2 medium carrots, finely chopped
2 celery stalks, finely chopped
2 large cloves garlic, crushed
1/2 teaspoon allspice (several pinches)

Salt and pepper, to taste
1 cup dry red wine
1 small can (6 ounces) tomato paste
2 cans (28 ounces each) crushed
tomatoes
A handful fresh flat-leaf parsley,
chopped (about 1/4 cup)
1 cup chicken broth
2 pounds penne rigate or fat
rigatoni, cooked until al dente
when ready to serve

In a big sauce pot, heat oil over medium heat and brown meats. Skim off fat and add vegetables and garlic; cook until tender. Add allspice and salt and pepper to taste. Add remaining ingredients except pasta. Bring sauce to a boil, reduce heat to low, and simmer 30 minutes. Toss cooked pasta with half the sauce and transfer to serving bowls. Ladle remaining sauce on top of pasta and serve.

Roast Leg of Lamb with Mint Sauce

Feeds 8 to 12

1 large leg of lamb, boned and
completely defatted by butcher,
but not tied, 7 to 8 pounds, total,
once boned
1/4 cup extra-virgin olive oil
(a couple good glugs)

Montreal Steak Seasoning (by
McCormick) or coarse salt and
pepper, to taste
8 cloves garlic, smashed
1 bundle fresh mint from produce
section or 6 sprigs rosemary
(depending on your tastes)

Preheat oven to 400°F.

Rub lamb all over with oil. Generously season inside and out with Montreal Seasoning or coarse salt and pepper. Place garlic and mint or rosemary onto cut, boned side and fold roast over in half, as if hinged. Place on rack in roasting pan and slide into hot oven. Cook 15 minutes, reduce heat to 350°F and cook 60 minutes, or just until meat thermometer reads 140°F; begin checking every 5 minutes after 45 minutes. For medium-well roast, cook 150°F to 155°F. Let rest on carving board under aluminum foil tent for 20 minutes before carving.

Mint Sauce

1/2 cup chicken broth
1 cup fresh mint leaves (1 bundle)
3 tablespoons white wine vinegar
(3 splashes)

2 tablespoons extra-virgin olive oil
(a glug)
Dash pepper
2 pinches salt

Pulse all ingredients in blender or food processor till combined and serve with lamb.

Baked Stuffed Flounder

Feeds 8 to 12.

1 stick (8 tablespoons) butter
1 large onion, finely chopped
3 stalks celery, diced
2 cloves garlic, minced
1/2 red bell pepper, finely diced
4 cans (6 ounces each) crabmeat
1 teaspoon salt (eyeballed in
your palm)
1 teaspoon pepper (eyeballed)
1/2 teaspoon ground thyme
(eyeballed)

8 slices toasted, buttered, good-
quality white bread, diced
A palmful of fresh flat-leaf parsley,
chopped (2 tablespoons), plus
additional, for garnish
6 pounds flounder fillets, rinsed
and patted dry, sprinkled lightly
with salt
Softened butter
2 lemons, in wedges, for garnish

Preheat oven to 375°F.

Melt butter in skillet over medium heat and add vegetables and garlic. Sauté until tender. Combine salt, pepper, and thyme. Set aside. Add crabmeat and cook 3 minutes, then sprinkle with seasoning mixture. Mix in bread and parsley.

Place a mound of stuffing across half a fillet and fold other half over, as if hinged. Place stuffed flounder in lightly greased baking dish and spread a touch of softened butter over tops. Bake 18 to 20 minutes, until fish is cooked through. Garnish with additional chopped parsley and serve with lemon wedges.

Side Dishes

Mashed Potatoes

Feeds 8 to 12

5 pounds medium potatoes, peeled
   and quartered
$^1/_2$ stick (4 tablespoons) butter

$^1/_2$ cup heavy (whipping) cream or
   half-and-half
Salt and pepper, to taste

Put potatoes in a large pot and cover with water. Bring to a boil over high heat. Cook 20 minutes, until potatoes break easily with fork. Drain potatoes and return pot with potatoes to stove, placed over low heat to dry out pan. Mash potatoes with butter and cream until they are as smooth as you like, then add salt and pepper to taste.

VARIATIONS:

Garlic Mashed Potatoes

Sauté 4 cloves minced garlic in the $^1/_2$ stick butter over low heat for 3 minutes. Add to the potatoes with the cream. Sprinkle a little chopped parsley into garlic potatoes with your salt and pepper.

Sour Cream and Chive Mashed Potatoes

Substitute $^3/_4$ cup sour cream for the $^1/_2$ cup cream. Add 10 blades chopped fresh chives to potatoes with the salt and pepper.

Herbed Mashed Potatoes

Sauté 3 minced shallots in 1 tablespoon extra-virgin olive oil. Add to potatoes with butter and cream. Combine 2 tablespoons each finely chopped fresh thyme, sage, and rosemary with mashed potatoes until evenly distributed.

Stuffed Tomatoes

Feeds 8 to 12.

3 cups Italian bread crumbs
1/2 cup Kalamata olives, pitted and
    chopped
A handful grated Parmigiano cheese
    (1/4 cup)

2 cloves garlic, minced
2 pinches ground pepper
6 tablespoons extra-virgin olive oil
12 medium vine-ripe, firm tomatoes
1 lemon, halved

Preheat oven to 500°F.

Combine everything in a bowl except the tomatoes and lemon. Cut a sliver off the bottoms of tomatoes. Seed the tomatoes by cutting off the top third, then gently squeezing, upside down, over sink. Squeeze juice of lemon halves over seeded tomatoes and fill each tomato with a good scoop of stuffing, slightly mounded. Cook for 5 minutes on top rack of oven, until bread crumbs are crisp on top.

Jeffrey's Cauliflower au Gratin

Feeds 8 to 12.

2 heads cauliflower, rinsed and
    separated into florets
6 tablespoons butter
1 small onion, minced
4 tablespoons all-purpose flour
    (a handful), for sprinkling

2 1/2 cups milk
Salt and pepper, to taste
2 pinches ground nutmeg
1 pound sharp cheddar cheese,
    shredded

Steam cauliflower, sprinkled with a pinch of salt, in an inch of water brought to a boil then reduced to a simmer for 10 minutes, covered. Drain and set aside.

Preheat oven to 325°F and lightly grease a baking dish.

In a large skillet or deep pan, melt butter and sauté onion over medium-low heat for 5 minutes. Sprinkle with a little flour and cook a minute more. Add milk and cook until milk begins to thicken. Add salt and pepper and 2 pinches nutmeg. Stir in cheese until it melts. Add cauliflower and coat. Pour into baking dish and bake 30 minutes. Yum. (If Jeffrey's coming for dinner, double the recipe.)

Nanny's Bourbon-Baked Beans

Feeds 8 to 12.

Dried beans take several hours to cook. At the holidays, you need the oven for roasting meats and sides dishes at various temperatures. Using Nanny's recipe, which calls for canned beans, you'll get the beans done in only 45 minutes, saving the precious time and oven space. You'll never know the difference.

1/4 pound slab bacon, chopped
1 medium onion, minced
2 tablespoons Dijon mustard
3 tablespoons dark molasses
2 tablespoons dark brown sugar
  (a palmful)

1 jar (8 ounces) mango chutney,
  chopped
6 cans (15 1/2 ounces each) Great
  Northern Beans, drained and rinsed
Salt and pepper, to taste
1/4 cup bourbon

Preheat oven to 375°F.

Heat skillet and cook bacon over medium heat until fat begins to render. Add onion, and cook 1 minute. Add mustard, molasses, sugar, and chutney and heat to thin. Remove from heat. Pour beans into baking dish or bean pot and cover with mixture; combine until evenly coated. Season with salt and pepper. Bake 45 to 50 minutes, stirring in bourbon after 30 minutes and returning to oven for the last 15 to 20.

Baked Eggplant Rollettes

Feeds 8 to 12.

2 medium eggplants
Flour, for dredging
2 large eggs, beaten
Extra-virgin olive oil
1/2 pound thinly sliced mozzarella
2 cups ricotta, part skim, mixed with

2 tablespoons chopped fresh
  parsley (a palmful) and a pinch of
  ground nutmeg
2 cups Quick Marinara (recipe follows)
1/2 cup grated Parmigiano cheese
  (a couple of handfuls)

Preheat oven to 350°F.

Slice eggplant in 1/4-inch pieces lengthwise. Dredge in flour, coat in egg, and fry in 1/4 inch of hot oil over medium heat until golden, 4 minutes on each side. Drain on paper towels. Top with a slice of mozzarella and a small mound of the ricotta mixture, then roll up. Place a cup of sauce in baking dish and set rollettes into it. Pour more sauce over the top and cover with Parmigiano. Bake for 20 minutes.

Quick Marinara

Feeds 8 to 12.

4 cloves garlic, minced
2 tablespoons extra-virgin olive oil
2 pinches crushed red pepper flakes
2 sprigs chopped fresh oregano
A palmful fresh flat-leaf parsley,
    chopped

A few leaves fresh basil, torn
2 cans (28 ounces each) crushed
    tomatoes
A pinch ground cinnamon (for egg
    plant recipe only)

Cook garlic in oil with pepper flakes over medium heat until it speaks by sizzling in oil. Add herbs and tomatoes, and the pinch of cinnamon. Simmer over low heat 10 minutes.

Baby Carrots with Honey and Curry

Feeds 8 to 12.

4 bags (12 ounces each) baby carrots
1/2 stick (4 tablespoons) butter
1/4 cup honey (4 drizzles from dripper)

1/2 teaspoon curry powder (eye-
    balled in your palm)
1/4 teaspoon coarse salt (a couple
    pinches)

Steam carrots 5 minutes in an inch of water, covered, or until tender. Drain. Melt butter with honey and curry powder and salt. Toss with carrots and serve.

Braised Spinach with Nutmeg

Feeds 8 to 12.

Three 1-pound bags triple-washed
    spinach, stems removed, leaves
    rinsed but not dried

1/2 teaspoon ground nutmeg
Coarse salt, to taste

Place a third of the spinach in a big skillet over medium-low heat and turn until wilted. The water clinging to rinsed spinach will be enough to keep the pan damp but not wet while it's wilting. Continue to add spinach, as much as pan will hold, until all of the greens are wilted. Sprinkle with nutmeg and coarse salt and serve.

Green Beans

Feeds 8 to 12

3 pounds fresh green beans,
 trimmed and washed
1/4 stick (2 tablespoons) butter,
 melted

2 tablespoons extra-virgin olive oil
1 small onion, minced
Salt and pepper, to taste

Steam beans in an inch of water, covered, for 5 minutes or until tender but still bright green. Drain. In a skillet, melt butter in oil; add onion and cook for 5 minutes over medium heat. Toss with beans and season with salt and pepper, to taste.

VARIATIONS:

With mint: Add 4 tablespoons finely chopped fresh mint to butter mixture.
With parsley: Add 4 tablespoons chopped fresh parsley to butter mixture.
With almonds: Top beans with 4 ounces toasted, sliced almonds.

Butternut Squash with Maple Syrup

Feeds 8 to 12

4 medium butternut squash
1/2 stick (4 tablespoons) butter
1/2 cup maple syrup
1/4 teaspoon ground nutmeg

Salt and pepper, to taste
1/4 cup toasted chopped pecans, to
 garnish

Preheat oven to 400°F.

 Roast whole squash in upper oven until tender when pricked with fork, about 30 minutes. Split squash in half lengthwise when cool enough to touch and scoop out seeds. Cut across squash halves in half again. Place squash servings on large nonstick cookie sheet. Melt butter, then stir in syrup and nutmeg. Baste squash generously with this mixture. Sprinkle squash with salt and pepper and roast until browned, basting occasionally, another 30 minutes. Transfer butternut pieces to platter and sprinkle with toasted pecans to garnish.

Yams with Brazil Nuts

Feeds 8 to 12

1/2 stick (4 tablespoons) butter
1/4 teaspoon ground ginger
   (a couple pinches)
1/2 teaspoon ground nutmeg
   (double the ginger)
1/4 cup dark brown sugar

6 large yams, peeled and cut in half
   across
Zest of 1 orange
1/2 cup toasted and chopped
   brazil nuts

Preheat oven to 350°F.

Melt butter with ginger, nutmeg, and brown sugar over medium-low heat until sugar dissolves. With tongs, coat each piece of yam, then place in a baking dish. Roast 30 minutes. Top with orange zest and toasted nuts and serve.

Ratatouille

Feeds 8 to 12

3 cloves garlic, minced
1/4 teaspoon crushed red pepper
   (a couple of pinches)
3 tablespoons extra-virgin olive oil
   (3 times around the pan)
1 red bell pepper, seeded and
   chopped
1 green bell pepper, seeded and
   chopped
1 large yellow-skinned Spanish
   onion, peeled and chopped
1 medium eggplant, chopped

2 medium zucchini, chopped in
   large dice
20 Kalamata olives, pitted and
   coarsely chopped
3 tablespoons (a palmful) capers
Kosher salt, to taste
1 can (15 ounces) diced tomatoes
1 can (15 ounces) crushed tomatoes
A handful fresh flat-leaf parsley,
   chopped
One 3-ounce jar toasted pine nuts
   (pignoli) toasted in oven until
   golden

In a deep skillet or pot, working over medium heat, simmer garlic and crushed pepper in oil until the garlic speaks. Add bell peppers, onion, eggplant, zucchini, olives, capers, and kosher salt. Cover pan, reduce heat to medium-low, and cook the vegetables down, stirring occasionally, until eggplant begins to break down, about 10 to 15 minutes.

Add tomato products and parsley and heat through. Let stand until ready to serve. Transfer to serving dish and top with toasted nuts.

Dinner at Eight

More of Your Favorites from *The 30-Minute Meal*

More 30-Minute Meals

About *30-Minute Meals*. I have to say it makes me happy to see that these recipes continue to be so well-received. I am proud to share something that really makes our days and lives a little nicer.

This particular collection of *30-Minute Meals* is designed to do double duty. Try these meals first as simple suppers to get the feel of them. Then, entertain with them. They are easy, elegant, and make great menus for small, special gatherings.

I am passionate about entertaining in small groups. I was born a little too late to enjoy the era of the supper club. I daydreamed about it as a teenager—the intimacy of small, candlelit tables, Sinatra songs, quiet conversation, food served on plain white plates and pretty cocktails poured into dainty glasses. What a lush life!

This mood can be recaptured. Surprise a few friends (or one very special friend) with a weeknight invitation. If you're married, have a date in your own living room. With these time-friendly meals, you can "indulge" any night of the week. Play some pretty sounds on your stereo and light a couple of candles. Spoil yourself and those you really love one night soon.

Thank you for bringing the *30-Minute Meal* to life in your kitchens. Enjoy the new recipes!

All feed 4 to 6 unless otherwise noted.

Pasta

Pasta is my favorite way to fill a belly. Judging from all the requests I get for more pasta meals, it's the meal of choice for many of you as well.

Pasta alla Norma

Feeds 4 to 6.

I call this classic Sicilian dish Pasta alla Norma because of the calming effect it had on my mother as I watched her eat it three nights in a row at Café Andrea in Amalfi.

1 cup extra-virgin olive oil (You will not ingest most of this, so don't flip out.)

5 or 6 baby eggplants, halved and sliced crosswise 1/2 inch thick

Salt and pepper, to taste

4 cloves garlic, minced

2 cans (28 ounces each) San Marzano or other whole tomatoes, drained, seeded, and diced (see Note)

1 can (14 ounces) crushed tomatoes

10 leaves fresh basil, torn, plus a few whole leaves for garnish

4 ounces crumbled ricotta salata cheese (Look in international cheese case of market.)

1 pound pennette or penne rigate, cooked until al dente

Heat three-quarters of the oil in deep skillet over medium heat. Add half the eggplant and gently fry until tender and golden. Transfer eggplant to paper–towel lined plate to drain, then repeat with more eggplant. Sprinkle eggplant with salt and pepper.

Drain and wash pan, dry, and return to stove. Heat remaining oil over medium heat with garlic until garlic speaks by sizzling in oil. Add drained and seeded diced tomatoes and crushed tomatoes. Stir in torn basil leaves. Allow sauce to bubble and thicken for 10 minutes.

Toss two-thirds of sauce with eggplant, crumbled cheese, and pasta. Transfer this to serving platter and cover with remaining sauce. Bread. Wine.

Note: If you cannot get San Marzano tomatoes, sprinkle another brand with 2 pinches sugar.

Baglio Della Luna Marinara

Feeds 4.

Dinner in Agrigento at the Baglio Della Luna as the kitchen was closing: "I'll take anything you have left," I said in very bad Italian. This fantastic dish was what I got.

3 tablespoons extra-virgin olive oil
(3 times around the pan)
4 cloves garlic, minced
3 pinches crushed red pepper
2 cans (6 ounces each) Italian tuna
in oil, drained or 2 cans (6
ounces each) Albacore tuna,
drained
1 cup dry red wine, a few good glugs
1 can (14 ounces) diced tomatoes
and 1 can (14 ounces) crushed
tomatoes

16 to 20 oil-cured black olives, pitted
and coarsely chopped
2 tablespoons capers, smashed with
flat of knife
A handful fresh flat-leaf parsley,
chopped (2 tablespoons)
A few grinds black pepper
1/2 pound penne, cooked until al
dente

In a deep skillet, heat olive oil, garlic, and crushed red pepper over medium heat until garlic speaks by sizzling in oil. Add tuna and sauté a minute or two. Add wine, bring to a boil, and reduce liquid by half. Add crushed tomatoes, olives, capers, parsley, and a few grinds of black pepper. Bring to a bubble, reduce heat, and simmer 10 minutes. Toss pasta in two-thirds of sauce and transfer to platter. Serve with remaining sauce for passing, and salad and bread.

Wildly Delicious
Wild Mushroom Fettuccine

Feeds 4 to 6.

1/4 cup extra-virgin olive oil (4 quick turns around the pan in thin stream)

2 shallots, minced

2 portobello mushroom caps, halved and thinly sliced

6 crimini mushroom caps, halved and thinly sliced

6 shiitake mushroom caps, slivered

1/4 teaspoon ground thyme (4 pinches)

2 pinches ground nutmeg

Coarse salt and a few grinds black pepper, to taste

1/2 cup good sherry

1 cup chicken broth

2/3 cup heavy (whipping) cream (4 trips around pan in slow and steady stream)

1 pound egg fettuccine, cooked until al dente

1/2 cup toasted chopped hazelnuts, for garnish (optional)

6 blades fresh chives, for garnish

Grated Romano or pepato cheese, for table

Heat olive oil in a large skillet over medium heat. Add shallots, sauté 2 minutes, then add mushrooms. Sauté mushrooms 2 minutes, then cover pan, reduce heat to medium-low, and cook until juices are extracted and mushrooms are dark and tender, another 3 to 5 minutes. Uncover and raise heat back to medium. Add thyme, nutmeg, salt, and pepper. Toss mushrooms with a good shake of the pan. Add sherry and reduce liquid by half, 2 or 3 minutes. Add broth, then cream. Simmer until sauce thickens so that it coats back of spoon, about 5 minutes. Toss with hot pasta and top with chives and toasted hazelnuts. Serve with crusty bread, grated cheese, and a green salad.

Tortellini with Gorgonzola and Walnut Sauce

Feeds 4.

1 family-size package (14-16 ounces) meat-filled tortellini
1 cup chicken broth

8 ounces Gorgonzola cheese
A pinch salt and a few grinds pepper
1 cup chopped toasted walnuts

Cook tortellini according to directions on package.

While tortellini is cooking, combine broth, cheese, salt, and pepper in a small saucepan and simmer over medium heat until cheese melts, about 2 minutes.

Toss pasta with sauce and walnuts. Serve with a spinach salad and warm bread.

Peasant Pasta

Feeds 4 to 6.

Only 5 ingredients, and nothing but raves. Enjoy.

1 pound bulk Italian sweet sausage
One 28-ounce can chunky-style crushed tomatoes

$1/2$ cup frozen green peas
$1/2$ cup heavy cream or half-and-half
$1/2$ pound penne rigate, cooked until al dente

Brown sausage and drain fat. Wipe out pot and return to heat. Add cooked sausage crumbles back to pot, with tomatoes. Bring to a bubble and cook together for 5 minutes. Add peas and cook for 1 minute more. Stir in cream, to blush the color of the sauce. Simmer until pasta is ready to drain. Toss two-thirds of the sauce with pasta and transfer to serving bowl. Top with remaining sauce and serve with grated cheese, crusty bread, and a bottle or two of Sangiovese wine.

Chicken and Rosemary Cream Rigatoni

Feeds 4 to 6.

SAUCE
4 cloves garlic, minced
1 large shallot, minced
2 tablespoons extra-virgin olive oil
1/2 cup dry white wine
1 1/2 cups no-fat, low-sodium, chicken broth
1/2 cup heavy (whipping) cream (3 or 4 times around the pan in slow stream)
3 sprigs fresh rosemary, leaves stripped from stem and finely chopped
A pinch ground nutmeg
Salt and pepper, to taste

1 pound chicken tenders, each cut in half across, or boneless, skinless breasts, cut into chunks
Balsamic vinegar (a couple of splashes)
Coarse salt and black pepper, to taste
1 tablespoon extra-virgin olive oil

1/2 pound penne rigate pasta, cooked until al dente
Grated Parmigiano or Romano cheese, for the table

In a large skillet or saucepan, cook garlic and shallots in olive oil over medium heat until garlic speaks by sizzling in oil. Add wine and reduce by half. Add chicken broth, cream, and seasonings. Cook over medium heat, stirring occasionally, 10 to 15 minutes, until sauce thickens.

While sauce simmers, rub chicken with a little balsamic vinegar, salt, and pepper. Heat olive oil in a second skillet over medium-high heat. Add chicken and cook 4 minutes on each side. Remove from heat.

Add chicken to thickened sauce and cook for 4 or 5 minutes. Toss with pasta and serve with plenty of grated cheese for topping and a tossed salad.

Mamma's Broccolini and Ricotta Pasta

Feeds 4 to 6.

Broccolini is an item that just appeared in the produce section one day. Science and progress can't be as scary as I thought, since they've come up with bundles of florets with no tough stalks. Broccolini—all florets, no thick stalks, less chopping. You get what you pay for. A way-cool thing.

2 bundles (3 cups) chopped broccolini florets or 2 heads broccoli rabe tops, chopped
1 cup water
2 tablespoons extra-virgin olive oil (twice around the pan)
1 pound skinless, boneless chicken breasts, diced
4 cloves garlic, minced

1 pound rigatoni, cooked until al dente, 1 cup of boiling water reserved
2 cups (1 pound) part-skim ricotta cheese
6 to 8 sprigs fresh thyme, leaves stripped from stem and chopped
A couple pinches ground nutmeg
Coarse salt and pepper, to taste

Simmer broccolini in a cup of water, covered, for 5 minutes, then drain. If using broccoli rabe, simmer for 8 to 10 minutes to extract bitterness. Drain well. Heat oil in big, deep skillet over medium heat. Add chicken and garlic. Cook for 5 to 8 minutes or until chicken is cooked through. Add broccolini or rabe, pasta, ricotta, the 1 cup cooking water from pasta, thyme, nutmeg, and salt and pepper to the pan. Toss until creamy, then transfer to a serving platter. Serve with a tomato and onion salad and crusty bread.

Penne with Saltimbocca Sauce

Feeds 4 to 6.

2 tablespoons butter
2 tablespoons extra-virgin olive oil
2 shallots, finely chopped
6 leaves fresh sage, piled and
    slivered (about 2 tablespoons)
2 bunches arugula, washed, dried,
    and chopped (2 cups)
Salt and pepper, to taste

2 pinches ground nutmeg
1 cup chicken broth
1/4 pound prosciutto di Parma ,
    chopped
1 pound penne or penne rigate,
    cooked until al dente
1/2 cup grated Parmigiano or
    Romano cheese

In a big, deep skillet, melt butter in oil over medium heat. Add shallots and sage and sauté 2 to 3 minutes. Add arugula and season with salt, pepper, and nutmeg. Pour in broth and bring to a bubble. Reduce heat to low and simmer, covered, until pasta is ready to drain.

To serve, remove cover and add prosciutto and pasta to pan. Toss with cheese and season with extra salt and pepper, if necessary, to taste.

Penne alla Rosa

Feeds 4 to 6.

Only 6 ingredients, and again, nothing but raves.

3 tablespoons extra-virgin olive oil
    (3 times around the pan)
2 cloves garlic, minced
1 small onion, peeled
One 28-ounce and one 14-ounce
    can crushed tomatoes
1/2 to 2/3 cup heavy cream or half-

and-half (4 turns around the pan
    in a slow, steady stream)
1 basil leaf
1 pound penne or pennette rigate,
    cooked until al dente
Grated Romano or Parmigiano
    cheese, for the table

Heat oil and garlic in deep skillet over medium heat. Grate onion into the pot with handheld grater. Sauté 5 minutes, stirring frequently. Add tomatoes and bring to a bubble. Add cream and basil. Bring to a bubble, reduce heat, and simmer 10 minutes. Toss two-thirds sauce with pasta, then transfer to platter or bowl. Top with remaining sauce and serve with green salad, bread, and grated cheese for the table.

Fradiavolo Sauce

Feeds 4 to 6.

Use this sauce for ANY seafood pasta supper. Add steamed mussels, seared scallops, lobster meat, clams, chunked fish, shrimp—whatever floats your fishing boat—to sauce and simmer a couple of minutes to combine flavors; toss with pasta of choice.

For topping 1 pound of pasta:
3 tablespoons extra-virgin olive oil
6 cloves garlic, minced
4 to 6 pinches crushed red pepper
   flakes (1/4 teaspoon) to your taste
2 sprigs fresh oregano, pulled off
   stems and finely chopped
   (1 tablespoon)

1/2 cup good sherry (a couple
   big glugs)
2 cans (28 ounces each) crushed
   tomatoes
Salt and pepper, to taste
A handful fresh flat-leaf parsley,
   chopped (1/4 cup)

Heat oil, garlic, and crushed red pepper in a deep skillet over medium heat. Cook until garlic speaks by sizzling in oil. Add oregano and give the pan a shake. Add sherry and reduce liquid by half, a minute or two. Add tomatoes, salt and pepper to taste, and the handful of chopped parsley. Simmer 10 minutes.

Seafood

I always feel as if I've done a good deed after eating seafood, especially on a Friday.

Broiled Cod and Amalfi-Coast Lemon Linguini

Feeds 4 to 6.

Amalfi is lemon flavored. The lemon trees are grown on terraced soil from the sea up to the sun. The lemons are as big as grapefruit here. The smell of citrus is always in the air. Mamma and I, we tried lemon everything—lemon liqueurs and lemon candy, lemon sodas and lemon ices—they even put lemons on pasta here!

We have tried to re-create this very rich creamy sauce. We paired it with a broiled piece of cod and the results are yummy and a real stunner for your guests or your family.

2¹/₂ pounds fresh cod (see Note), 1 inch thick (Don't let them give you tails.)
Coarse salt, to taste
2 tablespoons butter, softened
2 tablespoons good mayonnaise, sugar free, such as Hellmann's
¹/₄ cup water
Chopped fresh parsley or fresh chives to garnish
Lemon slices (optional), to garnish

Note: Fresh fish is firm and shows no signs of breaking.

AMALFI LEMON SAUCE
1 stick butter
8 tablespoons lemon juice (the juice of 4 lemons)
Zest of 3 lemons (2 tablespoons packed, grated rind)
1 cup heavy (whipping) cream
1 cup grated Parmigiano cheese
1 pound linguini or tagliatelle, cooked until al dente while cooking sauce
Salt and pepper, to taste
¹/₂ cup chopped fresh flat-leaf parsley (half a bunch)

Preheat broiler to 500°F.

Wash and dry fish. Sprinkle lightly with salt. Mix butter and mayonnaise and spread mixture over fish. Place a splash of water on a shallow pan and set fish on it. Set aside and start sauce.

In a large skillet, melt butter over medium-low heat. Add lemon juice and zest and simmer 3 or 4 minutes. Whisk in cream and half the cheese. Bring just to a simmer and remove from heat.

Place fish under broiler, 5 inches from heat, and cook 6 to 8 minutes, removing when golden and firm. Transfer fish carefully to serving plate and garnish with chives and lemon slices.

Toss drained al dente pasta with lemon sauce and salt and pepper to taste. Transfer to serving platter. Top pasta with remaining cheese and parsley.

Ginger Soy Salmon and Sesame Snap Peas

Feeds 4 to 6.

2 boxes (5 ounces each) curry couscous, prepared as directions on box, plus 2 tablespoons golden or dark raisins when water is added

2 to 2¹/2 pounds salmon fillet, 1 inch thick, no tail

¹/4 cup vegetable or peanut oil (a couple glugs)

¹/8 cup soy sauce (half as much as oil)

¹/4 palmful ground ginger (about 1 teaspoon)

1 cup water

1 pound sugar snap peas

2 green onions, thinly sliced, for garnish

1 tablespoon dark sesame oil (once around pan)

Coarse salt

Toasted sesame seeds, for garnish

Preheat oven to 425°F with a shallow metal pan placed on center rack.

Start couscous according to box directions.

Pat salmon dry and turn in oil combined with soy sauce and ginger.

Place water and snap peas in a covered skillet. Bring to a boil, reduce heat, and simmer 2 minutes. Drain peas and wipe skillet dry. Return skillet to stove.

Place salmon on the pan in the oven. Cook 10 minutes or until firm and opaque. Remove from oven and garnish with sliced green onions.

Heat sesame oil in skillet over medium-high heat till it smokes. Add peas and stir-fry for 2 or 3 minutes. Remove from heat and sprinkle with coarse salt and a little sesame seed.

To serve, cut fish into 4 to 6 servings and lift up and away from skin with a spatula. Place a chunk of fish on plate alongside a generous scoop of couscous and a few sugar snap peas.

Shrimp Scampi

Feeds 4 to 6.

2 pounds large, raw shrimp, peeled and deveined under running water, butterflying as you devein by cutting lengthwise into shrimp, almost splitting them

1 cup all-purpose flour

2 teaspoons (half a palmful) ground thyme or Old Bay seasoning

Coarse salt and freshly ground black pepper, to taste

1/2 cup extra-virgin olive oil (4 or 5 times around the pan)

6 cloves garlic, popped from skin and minced

1 cup dry white wine (a couple good glugs)

1 large lemon

1 cup canned chicken broth (about the same amount as wine)

A couple drops Worcestershire sauce

3 tablespoons butter (a few pats)

A handful fresh flat-leaf parsley, finely chopped

Pat shrimp dry with paper towels. Mix flour with a little ground thyme or Old Bay seasoning, salt, and pepper in a shallow dish. Lightly coat shrimp in seasoned flour. Pour olive oil into a deep, heavy-bottomed skillet placed over high heat. Cook shrimp in a single layer, in 2 batches if necessary. Sauté each batch 2 or 3 minutes, until edges are golden. Remove shrimp from skillet and place on paper towel–lined plate. Pour off any excess oil. Return pan to heat. Add garlic to pan. Add the wine to the pan and scrape up any good bits from the bottom. Reduce wine by half. Roll lemon on counter with a back-and-forth motion to release its juices. Split lemon in half. Add broth, Worcestershire, and the juice from the lemon halves. Let the sauce simmer for 2 or 3 minutes to reduce the liquids. Stir in butter with a whisk or fork.

Season sauce with more salt and pepper. Add the shrimp back to sauce and remove from heat. Give the pan a shake. Sprinkle with parsley and serve with crusty bread for dunking or pour over a bed of angel hair pasta cooked al dente—with a bite.

Italian Surf and Turf: Tenderloin Steaks and Fettuccine with Lobster Cream Sauce

Feeds 2.

6 tenderloin of beef steak
    medallions, ³/₄ inch thick
2 splashes balsamic vinegar
Montreal Steak Seasoning (by
    McCormick) or coarse salt and
    black pepper, to taste
Four 8-ounce lobster tails
¹/₂ stick (4 tablespoons) butter
2 tablespoons extra-virgin olive oil
    for lobster, plus drizzle for beef
4 cloves garlic, minced
1 cup dry white wine

A handful fresh flat-leaf parsley,
    finely chopped
1 can (28 ounces) crushed tomatoes
1 cup light cream or half-and-half
    (poured in a slow stream, 4 trips
    around the pan)
1 pound egg fettuccine, cooked
    until al dente
¹/₄ cup water (a splash)
Garlic bread or buttered toasted
    white bread, for garnish

Rub tenderloins with a little balsamic vinegar and sprinkle with seasoning; set aside.

Split shell on the belly side of lobster tails using strong scissors. Remove meat by sliding a long, thin knife between the shell and the meat to loosen meat. Cut lobster meat into bite-size chunks. Melt butter in olive oil in a skillet over medium to medium-high heat. Add lobster and cook 3 minutes on each side. Add garlic and cook another minute. Add white wine and give the pan a good strong shake or two. Reduce wine by half. Sprinkle pan with parsley, add tomatoes, and heat through. Add cream and combine until sauce is a light pink color. Reduce heat to low and let simmer.

Heat a nonstick skillet over high heat. Brush pan with a touch of olive oil. Place steaks in the hot pan and cook for 3 minutes on each side. Add a touch of water to the pan and pick up all the color off the bottom of the pan by turning the steaks in the juice. Remove from heat and let meat stand 5 minutes before serving to allow the juices to distribute.

When pasta is cooked until al dente (with a bite to it), drain it and cold-shock it by running it briefly under cold tap water to stop the cooking process. Shake out all of the water and drop the pasta into the sauce and toss.

To serve, place a steak on top of a slice of garlic bread or buttered toast. Pile some lobster cream sauce pasta alongside. Serve with a green salad tossed with olive oil and balsamic vinegar and enjoy!

Meats Made Easy

Meats and their preparation cause more anxiety than almost any other food group. All of the tips and tricks I know are worked into these recipes. As with all cooking, the most important tip is to relax.

Lamb Chops with Rosemary and Warm Cherry Tomato and Onion Salad

Feeds 4 to 6.

2 tablespoons extra-virgin olive oil (twice around the pan)
1 1/2 pounds thin-cut lamb rib chops (8 to 10 chops)
Montreal Steak Seasoning (by McCormick) or coarse salt and black pepper, to taste
2 cloves garlic, cracked from skin
4 sprigs fresh rosemary, leaves stripped from stem and chopped
1/2 cup dry white vermouth or dry white wine

SALAD
2 tablespoons extra-virgin olive oil
2 pints cherry tomatoes, cleaned and stems removed, 1 pint halved, 1 pint left whole
1 small onion, quartered and very thinly sliced
A handful chopped fresh flat-leaf parsley (1/4 cup)
Coarse salt and black pepper, to taste

Heat 1 tablespoon oil in a large, heavy-bottomed skillet over medium-high heat. Season chops with Montreal Seasoning or coarse salt and black pepper. Add half the chops and 1 clove garlic to pan when oil begins to smoke. Cook chops 3 minutes per side and remove to a plate. Repeat with next batch of chops. Add rosemary and cook half a minute in oil and meat bits. Add vermouth or wine and scrape up any good bits. Reduce 1 minute, then drizzle pan juices down over meat.

To make the salad, keep the pan over the same heat. Add olive oil. Add onion and cook for 1 minute. Add the tomatoes, both halved and whole. Give the pan a few good shakes and cook to just heat the tomatoes through, 2 or 3 minutes. Sprinkle with parsley and salt and pepper. Spoon alongside the lamb chops. Serve with warm crusty bread.

Pork Chops with Macerated Strawberries

Feeds 4 to 6.

1 pint fresh strawberries, thinly
   sliced
20 leaves fresh basil, piled, rolled
   into log, and thinly sliced
2 teaspoons sugar (half a palmful)
3 tablespoons balsamic vinegar
   (3 small splashes)
5 fresh figs, quartered (when in
   season)

1^1/$_2$ pounds boneless pork loin
   chops ^{1}/$_2$ to ^{3}/$_4$ inch thick
Balsamic vinegar
Coarse salt and black pepper or
   Montreal Steak Seasoning (by
   McCormick), to taste
1 tablespoon extra-virgin olive oil
   (once around the pan)
^{1}/$_4$ cup water (a couple good
   splashes)

Combine sliced berries and basil in a small bowl. Sprinkle with sugar and vine-gar and combine well. Add fresh figs, when in season, to this dish. Set the bowl aside and let stand.

Rub chops with a little of the vinegar and some Montreal Seasoning or coarse salt and pepper. Place a skillet over medium-high to high heat and lightly coat with olive oil. Place chops in hot pan and cook 4 minutes on each side. While chops cook, place a tent of aluminum foil over the center of the pan to reflect heat and allow steam to continue to escape from the pan. Turn chops only once. When chops have cooked for 8 minutes total, add a little water to the pan to lift up any pan juices and color. Cook till liquid evaporates, rubbing chops all around the pan.

Transfer chops to serving plate and let rest 5 minutes. Plate chops with a pile of macerated berries alongside and a serving of a lightly dressed salad of mixed greens. Pass extra berries and figs when you pass the bread.

Cashew! God Bless You. Pork Stir-Fry

Feeds 4.

2 cups jasmine rice (from Asian foods aisle), cooked following directions on box

1 cup fresh green beans (a handful), cut in halves

1/2 cup water

1 tablespoon peanut or vegetable oil

1 pound pork tenderloin, cut into 1/4-inch slices

1/3 cup (a few rounded tablespoonfuls) hoisin sauce (available on Asian foods aisle)

1/3 cup all-fruit apricot spread (a few rounded tablespoonfuls)

Juice of 1 orange

1 tablespoon dark sesame oil (once around the pan)

1/2 red bell pepper, cut in half lengthwise then thinly sliced across

1 cup drained bamboo shoots (a couple handfuls)

1/3 cup (a couple of palmfuls) roasted unsalted cashews (from the bulk bin in market)

Start rice cooking.

In a small pan, steam green beans in 1/2 cup water for 5 minutes, covered. Run under cold water in colander to cool. Drain and set aside.

Heat large skillet over medium-high heat. Add peanut or vegetable oil and heat until smoking. Add pork medallions and stir-fry 3 or 4 minutes. Remove from pan to plate. Cover with aluminum foil tent.

Mix hoisin sauce, apricot spread, and orange juice. Return pan to heat and add 1 tablespoon sesame oil. When oil smokes, add vegetables and stir-fry 2 minutes. Add sauce mixture and give the pan a good shake. Return pork to pan. Sprinkle pan with nuts and toss to coat everything evenly with sauce. Serve several large spoonfuls of cashew pork over a mound of jasmine rice. Yum.

Smoked Pork Chops with Apple and Onion

Feeds 4 to 6.

2 large sweet onions, peeled and
   thinly sliced
3 tablespoons butter
1 tablespoon vegetable oil (once
   around the pan) plus a drizzle for
   pork chops

2 large green apples, thinly sliced
A pinch ground nutmeg
1 1/2 pounds (6 to 8 chops) smoked
   pork chops
A pinch each salt and pepper

In a deep skillet over medium-high heat, cook onions in butter and a touch of oil until onions are very soft and caramelized. Add apples and cook another minute or two. Sprinkle pan with a pinch of nutmeg and remove from heat.

Pan-fry pork chops in a little oil over medium-high heat for 3 minutes on each side. Season with a pinch of salt and a touch of freshly ground pepper.

Place chops on serving platter and cover completely with apples and onions. Serve with buttered corn toastees and collard greens or spinach.

Veal Scallopini with Wild Mushrooms

Feeds 4 to 6.

1 1/2 pounds thin veal shoulder
   scallopini
1/2 cup all-purpose flour
1/2 teaspoon poultry seasoning or
   ground thyme (a couple pinches)
Salt and pepper, to taste
3 tablespoons butter, cut in small
   pieces
2 tablespoons extra-virgin olive oil
   (twice around the pan)
3 cloves garlic, popped from skin
12 crimini mushroom caps, thinly
   sliced

2 portobello mushroom caps,
   thinly sliced
6 shiitake mushroom caps, slivered
4 sprigs fresh rosemary, leaves
   stripped from stems and finely
   chopped
1 cup dry white vermouth or dry
   white wine
1 cup beef broth
1 tablespoon balsamic vinegar
   (once around the pan)

Pat veal scallopini dry with paper towels. Combine flour in a shallow dish with poultry seasoning or ground thyme, and salt and pepper. Heat heavy-bottomed skillet over medium-high heat. Add half the butter and all the olive oil to the pan with the garlic cloves. Add veal in a single layer and cook for 2 to 3 minutes on each side, until pieces are lightly golden and cooked through. Transfer veal scallops to serving platter and repeat with remaining pieces. Cover platter loosely with aluminum foil and set aside.

Add mushrooms to pan, sprinkle with rosemary, and cook, stirring frequently, until mushrooms soften and have given off their juices. If mushrooms begin to stick before they soften, reduce heat a little. Add vermouth or wine and scrape up any good gunk from the bottom of the pan. Cook until wine almost evaporates. Add broth and reduce 5 minutes over medium-low heat. Stir in balsamic vinegar. Remove from heat and stir in remaining butter in small pieces. Spoon mushrooms and sauce evenly over veal scallops. Pass a few grinds of pepper over platter. Serve with pasta tossed with garlic and oil, or lots of crusty bread for sopping up the juices, and a nice mixed green or spinach salad.

Veal Piccata

Feeds 4 to 6.

1¹/₂ pounds very thin veal shoulder scallopini
¹/₂ cup all-purpose flour
¹/₂ teaspoon poultry seasoning or ground thyme (a couple pinches)
Salt and pepper, to taste
3 tablespoons butter, cut in small pieces
2 tablespoons extra-virgin olive oil (twice around the pan)

3 cloves garlic, minced
1 cup dry white vermouth or dry white wine
1 large lemon
2 tablespoons capers, smashed with flat of knife
A handful fresh flat-leaf parsley, chopped

Dust veal in flour combined with thyme, salt, and pepper. Heat a large skillet over medium-high heat. Melt half the butter in the oil and brown veal in a single layer 2 minutes on each side. Remove cooked veal to a platter and cover with loose aluminum foil. Repeat and remove cooked veal from pan and add to platter. Reduce heat to medium and add garlic. Shake pan and add vermouth or wine. Let liquid reduce by half and squeeze the juice of the lemon into pan. Whisk in remaining butter. Add capers and parsley and pour sauce over veal. Serve with bread or side dishes of garlic-oil pasta and spinach salad.

Veal Dumplings and Egg Fettuccine

Feeds 4 to 6.

1 pound ground veal
1 large egg
1 cup bread crumbs
1/2 small onion, grated
1/2 teaspoon ground nutmeg
1/2 cup grated Romano or
    Parmigiano cheese
Black pepper, to taste

2 tablespoons butter, cut into bits
4 sprigs fresh thyme, stripped from
    stems and chopped (about 2
    tablespoons)
2 cloves garlic, minced
One 28-ounce plus one 14-ounce can
    crushed tomatoes
Coarse salt, to taste
1 box (14 to 16 ounces) egg fettuc-
    cine, cooked until al dente

Heat a deep pot of water to a boil.

Combine veal and the next 6 ingredients. Roll veal into small 1/2-inch balls. Drop balls into pot of boiling water, reduce heat, and cook 12 minutes, covered. Drain. Return pan to heat.

In the same pot, melt butter over medium heat. Add thyme and garlic. When garlic speaks by sizzling in butter, add tomatoes and veal dumplings. Add coarse salt, to taste. Simmer 5 minutes. Drain cooked pasta and toss with veal dumplings and sauce.

Balsamic Chicken with Orange and Oregano Relish

Feeds 4 to 6.

ORANGE AND OREGANO RELISH
6 seedless navel oranges, peeled and chopped
1/2 small red onion, finely chopped
3 sprigs fresh oregano, leaves stripped from stems and finely chopped
1 teaspoon red wine vinegar (a splash)
1 tablespoon extra-virgin olive oil (once around the bowl)
Coarse salt and black pepper, to taste

BALSAMIC CHICKEN
1 1/2 to 2 pounds boneless, skinless chicken breasts (6 pieces)
1 tablespoon balsamic vinegar (a few shakes)
Coarse salt and black pepper, to taste
1 tablespoon extra-virgin olive oil (once around the pan)
1/4 cup water (a good splash)

Combine oranges, onion, oregano, red wine vinegar, olive oil, and salt and pepper in a bowl. Let the relish hang out at room temperature while you prepare the chicken.

Rub chicken breasts with balsamic vinegar and salt and pepper. Heat olive oil in a skillet or on a nonstick griddle over medium-high heat. Add chicken and cook 4 to 5 minutes on each side. To protect yourself from spatters and to speed up the cooking process, cover the pan very loosely with a little aluminum foil tent. Once you flip the chicken, give the opposite side a minute or two to brown, then add water to the pan and for the last 2 minutes, continue to move breasts around the pan to pick up all the beautiful color from the vinegar that is caramelizing the chicken. When the water evaporates, the chicken should be glossy and dark brown all over. Transfer to a serving dish and top each breast generously with orange relish. Serve with egg pasta tossed with butter and fresh parsley and a green salad.

Savannah Captain's Chicken

Feeds 4 to 6.

From the South, a dish said to have traveled to Georgia from the ports of Venice via a ship captain with a penchant for cooking.

2 pounds (6 pieces) boneless,
  skinless chicken breasts
1/2 cup all-purpose flour
Salt and pepper, to taste
1/4 cup extra-virgin olive oil
2 medium onions, chopped
1 red bell pepper, diced

1 clove garlic, minced
2 teaspoons curry powder (half a
  palmful)
1/2 teaspoon ground thyme (6 or 7
  pinches)
1 can (15 ounces) crushed tomatoes
A handful currants
1/4 cup sliced almonds, toasted

Dredge chicken in a shallow dish of flour seasoned with the salt and pepper. Heat oil over medium-high heat in a deep skillet. Brown chicken 4 minutes on each side, then remove. Add onions and bell pepper and cook 5 minutes. Add garlic, curry powder, and thyme. Give the pan a shake. Add tomatoes and currants. Return chicken to pan, cover, and reduce heat. Simmer till chicken is cooked through, another 3 to 5 minutes. Top with toasted nuts and serve right from pan with crusty French bread or rice and a green salad.

Lemon-Thyme Chicken with Sweet Gnocchi

Feeds 4.

4 tablespoons all-purpose flour (a handful)

$1/2$ teaspoon coarse salt (a few good pinches)

Freshly ground black pepper, to taste

$1/2$ teaspoon poultry seasoning (a couple pinches)

$1^1/2$ pounds boneless, skinless chicken breasts

3 tablespoons extra-virgin olive oil

2 tablespoons butter (2 pats)

1 medium onion, chopped

1 cup no-fat, low-sodium chicken broth

Juice of 2 lemons, rolled on counter to release juices

6 to 8 sprigs fresh thyme, leaves stripped from stem and chopped

SWEET GNOCCHI

1 pound potato gnocchi (found in frozen foods section), cooked following directions on package

2 tablespoons butter

$1/2$ teaspoon ground cinnamon (a couple pinches)

2 tablespoons sugar

Grated Parmigiano Reggiano cheese

While you're preparing the chicken, put water on the stove to boil for the gnocchi.

Dump flour, salt, pepper, and poultry seasoning in a big plastic Baggie. Pat chicken dry and drop into bag. Give the chicken a good shake to lightly coat the breasts. Remove chicken from the Baggie and set aside, saving the additional flour. Heat olive oil over medium-high heat in a big nonstick skillet. Add chicken and cook 5 minutes on the first side, flip, and cook another 5 minutes. Remove chicken and add a pat of butter and the onion to the pan. Cook 2 or 3 minutes, stirring frequently. Add reserved flour and cook 1 minute more to incorporate flour. Add broth and bring sauce to a boil. Reduce heat to medium-low and squeeze lemon juice into sauce. Add thyme and additional pat of butter. Add chicken back to pan and let simmer until gnocchi is done.

Toss hot gnocchi with a little butter. Mix the cinnamon into the sugar. Sprinkle cinnamon sugar over gnocchi and toss. Top with a generous sprinkling of Parmigiano cheese and serve alongside lemon-thyme chicken breasts. Steamed baby carrots make a nice accompaniment.

Northern Italian Stuffed Chicken

Serves 4.

2 tablespoons extra-virgin olive oil
   (twice around the pan)
1 small onion, minced
3 cloves garlic, minced
1/2 package (10 ounces) chopped
   spinach, defrosted and squeezed
   dry
A pinch each salt, pepper, ground
   nutmeg, and ground thyme
3 to 4 ounces ricotta salata cheese
   (from international cheese case),
   crumbled

4 boneless, skinless chicken breasts
Salt and pepper, to taste
1 cup chicken broth
1 lemon, skin zested into small dish,
   juice reserved
1 tablespoon cornstarch
A handful chopped fresh flat-leaf
   parsley, for garnish

Heat 1 tablespoon oil over medium heat in skillet. Sauté onion and garlic for 2 minutes, add drained spinach, and cook a minute more. Sprinkle with salt, pepper, nutmeg, and thyme. Remove from heat, cool, and add cheese to mixture.

Cut a horizontal slit in the thickest part of chicken breast, going in from the thick side. Stuff 2 rounded tablespoonfuls of stuffing into each breast.

Heat second teaspoon olive oil in a big skillet over medium-high heat. Sprinkle chicken with a little salt and pepper, to taste, and cook 6 minutes on each side. Remove from pan and add broth. Mix the lemon zest with the lemon juice and cornstarch, whisk into sauce, and cook 1 minute, until thick. Return chicken to pan and heat 1 minute more, coating chicken with sauce. Garnish with chopped fresh parsley and serve with crusty bread and a salad.

Chicken Chasseur with Herbed Egg Fettuccine

Feeds 4 to 6.

Everyone who tastes this, flips. It is a thirty-minute version of the classic French hunter's chicken.

1/4 teaspoon ground thyme (4 pinches)

Coarse salt and black pepper, to taste

1/2 cup all-purpose flour (a couple handfuls)

1 1/2 pounds boneless, skinless chicken breast cutlets, cut into large pieces (3 per breast)

2 tablespoons extra-virgin olive oil (twice around the pan)

2 tablespoons butter

8 to 10 baby carrots, thinly sliced

1 rounded teaspoon sugar

2 large shallots, minced

12 crimini mushroom caps, chopped

1 cup dry red wine (3 or 4 times around the pan in a slow stream)

1 can (28 ounces) crushed tomatoes

2 tablespoons chopped fresh tarragon leaves (4 sprigs)

3 tablespoons butter

1 large shallot, minced

12 blades fresh chives, chopped

A handful fresh flat-leaf parsley, chopped

1 pound fresh egg fettuccine, cooked

Mix thyme, salt, pepper, and flour in a dish. Coat chicken in flour and set aside. Discard flour. Heat oil and butter in large, deep skillet over medium heat. Brown chicken pieces for 4 minutes on each side and remove. Put carrots in pan, sprinkle with sugar, and cook for 1 minute. Add shallots and mushrooms and cook 3 to 5 minutes to soften. Add wine and reduce by half. Add tomatoes and tarragon and return chicken to pan. Give the pan a shake. Simmer until chicken is cooked through, another 3 to 5 minutes.

Melt butter and cook shallots 5 minutes over medium heat. Add herbs. Toss egg fettuccine with butter and herbs while still hot. Serve alongside chicken.

Tuscan Chicken

Feeds 4 to 6.

2 pounds boneless, skinless chicken breasts, quartered
1/3 cup (a handful) of all-purpose flour
Salt and pepper, to taste
1/4 teaspoon ground thyme (4 pinches)
3 tablespoons extra-virgin olive oil (3 times around the pan)
4 cloves garlic, cracked from skin, left whole

1/3 cup white wine vinegar
1 cup dry white wine
1 cup beef broth
6 sprigs fresh rosemary, leaves stripped from stem and finely chopped
2 to 3 tablespoons superfine flour (available on the baking aisle in a shaker can)
1 to 2 tablespoons warm water

Coat chicken with flour, salt, pepper, and thyme. Heat olive oil and garlic over medium-high heat until garlic speaks by sizzling in oil. Add chicken and brown for 4 minutes per side. Add vinegar and deglaze the pan, scraping up all the juicy bits. Cook vinegar down for 1 minute. Add the wine and reduce by half, about 3 minutes. Add broth and rosemary. Bring to a boil. Reduce heat and simmer over low heat for 5 to 7 minutes. Mix some superfine flour and water, a two-to-one ratio, in a cup. Add loose paste to sauce and thicken for a minute or two.

Serve right from the pot with hunks of crusty bread and a salad of tossed mixed greens.

Apricot-Glazed Chicken with Asian Green Beans

Feeds 4 to 6.

Kids love this, too. Make it at five for dinner, have guests at eight—anytime, it's great!

1¹/₂ pounds boneless, skinless chicken breasts, cut into chunks

1 tablespoon vegetable or peanut oil (once around the pan)

¹/₄ cup (3 or 4 good spoonfuls) hoisin sauce (available on Asian foods aisle)

1 cup all-fruit apricot preserves (3 or 4 good rounded spoonfuls)

Juice of 3 oranges

2 tablespoons low-sodium soy sauce, (a little splash or two)

2 green onions, thinly sliced, for garnish

1 cup white rice cooked in 2 cups water or ³/₄ pound spaghetti

ASIAN GREEN BEANS
³/₄ to 1 pound fresh green beans (4 big handfuls), trimmed and rinsed

¹/₂ cup water

2 tablespoons (twice around the pan) dark sesame oil, (available on Asian foods aisle)

2 oranges, halved

Coarse salt, to taste

Toasted sesame seeds (available on spice aisle)

Pat the chicken dry with paper towels. Heat the vegetable or peanut oil over medium-high heat until pan is very hot. Add chicken and cook 4 minutes on each side. With a whisk, combine hoisin, preserves, orange juice, and soy sauce in a dish. Remove chicken from the pan and add glaze mixture to pan. Allow glaze to bubble and reduce by half. Return chicken to the pan and coat the breasts with the thickened glaze. Pour chicken over rice, or toss with noodles for a lo-mein-like experience. Sprinkle with sliced green onions for garnish and serve with Asian green beans.

While chicken is cooking, steam green beans with water over high heat for 4 to 5 minutes in a covered skillet. Beans should be slightly tender but still crisp and bright green. Drain well. Return pan to high heat. Add sesame oil. When oil smokes, add green beans and pan-fry for 2 to 3 minutes, until edges darken and beans begin to crisp. Halve 2 oranges. Reserve a few thin slices for garnish. Squeeze the juice from the halves over the skillet. Toss the beans well. Sprinkle with coarse salt and remove from heat. Garnish with a generous sprinkle of toasted sesame seeds.

Tenderloin Steaks with Sweet Peppers and Potatoes

Feeds 4 to 6.

Six 4-ounce tenderloin steaks about 1-inch thick
Balsamic vinegar
1/4 cup brown sugar
1 1/2 tablespoons (half a palmful) Montreal Steak Seasoning (by McCormick)
1 tablespoon extra-virgin olive oil (once around the pan)

3 tablespoons butter
1 tablespoon extra-virgin olive oil (once around the pan)

2 cups Simply Potatoes diced potatoes with onions (available on dairy aisle). See Note.
1/2 red bell pepper, seeded and diced
1/2 green bell pepper, seeded and diced
1/2 yellow bell pepper, seeded and diced
Montreal Steak Seasoning (by McCormick) or salt and black pepper, to taste

6 toasted, buttered English muffins

Pat steaks dry with paper towels. Rub a little balsamic vinegar into meat. Combine brown sugar and seasoning blend in a small dish. Coat the steaks with the sugar and spice rub. Let stand while you begin potatoes.

In a deep skillet, melt butter with a touch of olive oil over medium-high heat. Add potatoes and cook until they begin to brown. Add peppers and seasoning and cook an additional 5 minutes, stirring occasionally.

While potatoes cook, heat olive oil over medium-high heat. Cook steaks 3 minutes on each side. Remove from heat and let stand 5 minutes.

Place 6 muffin halves on serving platter (to catch juices when cut through) and top with meat. Spill the peppers and potatoes into center of platter and around steak-topped muffins. Gorgeous—God, you are good. Serve with basket of remaining buttered muffin halves for passing at the table.

Note: These are fresh, precooked, diced potatoes, a great product. Each pouch (20 ounces) serves 6.

Three tips for great, tender steak:

• Have meat at room temperature before preparing your meal.

• Cook meat in a very hot pan 4 minutes on each side for an inch-thick steak, turning only with tongs. NEVER pierce meat when turning.

•Allow meat to rest before cutting so that juices can distribute evenly. If you cut into hot meat, the only bite that will taste good is the first.

Philly Steak Burritos

Feeds 4 to 6.

1¹/₄ to 1¹/₂ pounds flank or
    skirt steak
2 tablespoons balsamic vinegar or
    soy sauce
Montreal Steak Seasoning (by
    McCormick) or coarse salt and
    black pepper, to taste
A drizzle oil, to coat skillet

2 tablespoons extra-virgin olive oil
    (twice around the pan)
2 medium Spanish yellow-skinned
    onions, thinly sliced

2 medium green bell peppers,
    seeded and sliced
2 cloves garlic, minced
Montreal Steak Seasoning (by
    McCormick) or coarse salt and
    black pepper, to taste

Six 9-inch flour tortillas or flavored
    tortillas
6 tablespoons A1 or other steak
    sauce
Shredded cheddar or shredded
    smoked cheddar cheese (optional)

Pat steak dry with paper towels. Rub a little balsamic vinegar and the seasoning into the meat. Heat a griddle or nonstick skillet over high heat. Go once around the pan with oil, about 1 tablespoon, and wipe it around the surface of the pan with paper towels to coat lightly.

Place meat on skillet and cook 5 minutes on the first side, 4 on the flip side. Place a loose aluminum foil tent above meat while cooking. Remove steak from pan and let rest 5 minutes before slicing.

While meat is cooking, heat a second skillet over high heat. Add a little oil (twice around the pan). Add onions and peppers and cook, giving the pan a good shake often. Cook for 3 to 5 minutes, until vegetables are done to your taste. Add garlic and cook another minute, sprinkle with seasoning, and remove from heat.

Wipe the meat griddle clean and return to stove. Reheat pan over high heat and blister the tortillas for 30 seconds on each side. Pile the tortillas up on a cutting board or a plate.

To assemble, slice the meat very, very thin on an angle, against the grain. If the meat is not done enough for you, place the shavings briefly back on the hot griddle and give it a few quick tosses. Paint tortilla with a tablespoon of steak sauce and pile the meat down the center. Top with shredded cheese and a pile of peppers and onions. Tuck the top and bottom edges of the tortilla in, give the tortilla a quarter turn, and roll the burrito up. Cut in half and serve with oven fries and cold beer.

Sirloin Steak with Horseradish Cream and Warm German Potato Salad

Feeds 4.

2 pounds sirloin, cut into 2 steaks,
    each an inch thick
Worcestershire sauce

Montreal Steak Seasoning (by
    McCormick) or coarse salt and
    black pepper, to taste
A drizzle extra-virgin olive oil

Pat steaks dry with paper towels and brush with Worcestershire sauce. Sprinkle meats with seasoning and let rest a few minutes. Begin potato salad. (See the recipe following.)

To cook steaks, place a nonstick griddle or large skillet over medium-high heat. Add a drizzle of oil and heat until pan smokes. Add meat and cook 4 minutes on each side, placing aluminum foil tent over meat to reflect heat without trapping moisture. Remove from heat and let stand 5 minutes.

Slice thin, at an angle and against the grain. Serve an equal portion of sliced steak with a couple of spoonfuls of horseradish cream, French or whole-grain rolls, chunked tomato and cucumber salad, and Warm German Potato Salad.

Horseradish Cream

About 3/4 cup.

2 tablespoons prepared horseradish
1/2 cup sour cream or reduced-fat
    sour cream

1/4 cup heavy (whipping) cream
1/2 small onion, minced
8 blades fresh chives, finely chopped

Combine ingredients until smooth and spoon over meat when ready to serve.

Warm German Potato Salad

Feeds 4 to 6.

3 tablespoons butter

1 pouch (20 ounces) Simply
   Potatoes diced potatoes with
   onions (available on dairy aisle)
   See Note.

1 medium red onion, chopped

2 garlic cloves, minced

1/2 cup chicken broth

1/3 cup white vinegar or apple
   cider vinegar

1 teaspoon Dijon mustard

8 slices bacon, center cut or
   peppered, chopped, browned,
   drained on paper towels

Salt and pepper, to taste

Chopped fresh parsley and fresh
   dill, for garnish (2 to 3 tablespoons total)

Melt butter in large skillet over medium to medium-high heat and add potatoes. Cook, turning occasionally, until tender and lightly golden around edges. Add onion and garlic and cook 1 minute more. Mix broth, vinegar, and mustard. Pour over potatoes. Sprinkle pan generously with bacon. Shake pan or toss to combine, cooking a minute or two. Remove from heat and season with salt, pepper, parsley, and dill.

Note: These are fresh, precooked, diced potatoes, a great product. Each pouch serves 6. If you cannot find this product in your market, substitute 12 small white potatoes boiled till tender, 10 to 12 minutes, drained, and sliced or diced.

Bill's Sausage, Broccoli Rabe, and Pasta

Feeds 4 to 6.

When it's Bill Filiaci's night to cook for his family of five, this is a quick favorite that "fills the bill."

3 to 4 cloves garlic, minced

2 tablespoons extra-virgin olive oil
   (twice around the pan)

4 cups chopped broccoli rabe
   (rapini), the yield of 2 bunches

1 cup chicken broth

1 pound bulk Italian sweet sausage,
   browned and drained

1 pound penne rigate pasta, cooked
   until al dente

Salt and pepper, to taste

Grated Romano cheese, for the table

1/2 cup heavy (whipping) cream
   (optional)

Sauté garlic in olive oil over medium heat in a large, deep skillet until garlic speaks by sizzling in oil. Add broccoli rabe and cook until wilted, stirring frequently. Add broth and bring to a boil. Cover and reduce heat. Cook 10 minutes, or until florets are tender and no longer bitter. Add sausage and pasta, season with salt and pepper, and serve with a bowl of grated Romano for passing at the table.

VARIATION:

To make the dish richer, Bill adds cream after cooking broccoli rabe in broth. Bring cream to a bubble and let simmer until sauce thickens. Add sausage, pasta, and seasonings. Enjoy!

Beef Burritos Grande

Feeds 4 to 6.

1 tablespoon extra-virgin olive or corn oil (once around the pan)	Coarse salt, to taste
1 1/2 pounds lean ground beef	Six 9-inch flour tortillas or flavored flour tortillas
2 cloves garlic, minced	1 jar (8 ounces) mild taco sauce
1/2 small onion, chopped	Sour cream
1/2 medium red bell pepper, seeded and diced)	Shredded Monterey Jack, Pepper Jack, cheddar, or smoked cheddar cheese
1 1/2 tablespoons chili powder (half a palmful	Diced tomatoes
1 1/2 tablespoons ground cumin (half a palmful)	Chopped red onion
4 shakes cayenne pepper sauce	Shredded lettuce

Heat oil in skillet over high heat. Add beef and spread in an even layer. Brown beef for 2 minutes. Add garlic, onion, and bell pepper. Cook another 3 minutes. Add seasonings and a little coarse salt. Reduce heat to low and simmer.

Heat a second skillet or griddle over high heat. Blister the tortillas for 20 to 30 seconds on each side and pile up on a cutting board or a plate.

Paint center of tortilla with taco sauce and drop three dots of sour cream down center. Pile a little shredded cheddar onto tortilla and a cup or so of beef filling, working down the center, leaving a lip at each end. Top with tomatoes, onion, and shredded lettuce. Tuck the top and bottom of the tortilla in, give it a quarter twist, and roll burrito up. Split each burrito in half and serve with tortilla chips and a pitcher of margaritas.

Cooking Rookies

Kids Cook, Too

Never Too Young

People often ask me where and when I learned to cook. The truth is, I never did. No one "taught" me how to cook. No person ever showed me how to hold a knife or how to tell when chicken was done. No one explained to me which flavors were good together and which were not. How then did I learn? The answer has everything to do with my family.

The kitchen *was* the center of my childhood home. As kids, my brother and sister and I were spoiled in an unusual way. We were treated as respected members of the group. All the adults in the home, listened when we spoke, giving us the same attention they gave to other adults. In turn, when they spoke, we listened.

This is not to say that we were treated as adults. We were treated as children, with rules to follow, and were taught right from wrong. But, when given a direction to follow, we were spoken to in a way that assumed we were capable. "Rachael, clean the potatoes and add them to the pot, please," is a very different statement from "Rachael, can you clean the potatoes?" We were made to feel confident in our own abilities. We felt a responsibility to figure out how to do things for ourselves. I work with this in mind to this day. I look at the task at hand and say to myself, "I can figure this out." Then I get busy and figure it out.

Cooking can give kids a wonderful sense of accomplishment. They can see the results of their labors and creativity immediately—tangible, great-tasting food that others can share and enjoy. Kids develop a real sense of pride when given a pat on the back for something they did, all by themselves, despite their small size and age.

When it comes to ideas for your child's next party, cooking is cool! Gathering a group of kids together to cook is a triple treat for everyone. Activities are all taken care of—cooking is the name of this party game. Parents are happy because picky eaters aren't so picky when it's *their* food on the table. And at party's end, everyone has learned something not only about food, but something about themselves too. So, round up the troops and skip lunch, the *kids* are cooking tonight!

Easy-Cheesy Pizza Party

It's Dough-Easy

Makes 4 to 6 individual pies.

1/4 cup lukewarm water
1 package active dry yeast
A couple pinches sugar
3/4 to 1 teaspoon coarse salt
2 1/2 cups all-purpose unbleached

flour, plus a couple handfuls for kneading
1/4 cup extra-virgin olive oil (3 times around the bowl), plus a drizzle for oiling a large mixing bowl

In a big bowl, kids can combine the 1/4 cup water with the yeast and sugar. Set the bowl aside and let the mixture hang out for 10 minutes until it's all foamy and bubbly.

Kids, mix 1 cup of the flour with a couple of pinches of salt in a big bowl (don't forget to throw an extra pinch of salt over your left shoulder for luck!) Add the yeast mixture and stir with a big wooden spoon. Helpers can add the olive oil to the bowl, drizzling the oil 3 times around the bowl in a light stream. Kids add another cup of the flour to the bowl and keep stirring. When dough begins to form, remove the spoon and take turns working the flour in by hand—punch and roll and push the dough all around the bowl. This is called "kneading." Everybody can take turns kneading the dough. Kneading is the most important part, and the most fun! When you are kneading the dough by hand, you can feel whether or not you *need* all of your flour. If it is raining outside, your flour might have already sucked up some moisture right out of the air, so you might need only 2 1/4 cups. Stop kneading the dough when it is smooth and stretchy and no longer sticky.

Pour a little oil into a second big bowl and spread it around the sides of the bowl with a pastry brush (that's a paintbrush we use only in the kitchen). Dump the dough into the oiled bowl and turn it around until it is smooth and a little glossy and covered evenly with the oil. Now that the dough is as tired as you are, cover it up with a blanket made from a damp kitchen towel and let it take a nap. (This would be a great time for a juice break.) Helpers turn the oven on to 200°F for 5 minutes, then turn it off and put the covered bowl on a potholder-pillow placed on the center rack. Close the oven and let the dough rise till double in size, about 1 hour.

While the dough grows, kids can get the toppings ready and clean up the bowls and countertops with the Helpers.

"Helpers" refers to grown-up kids; we need them to handle the hot and the sharp things in life till we grow bigger than they are.

As soon as the dough comes out of the oven, preheat a pizza stone on the bottom rack of the oven at 500°F for 45 minutes.

Pepper-Pepperoni Pizza

Makes four 6-inch or two 8-inch pies or 1 large pie.

In Italy, *pepperoni* means "little peppers." If you order a pepperoni pizza in Rome, you would get a spicy surprise! The thinly sliced sausage we call pepperoni is made with crushed, dried little red peppers called pepperoncini. Pepper-Pepperoni Pizza is yummy because it combines big, sweet red peppers with spicy slices of pepperoni sausage and real, fresh mozzarella—the best pizza cheese you've ever eaten!

1 recipe It's Dough-Easy
A handful all-purpose flour to roll out
   dough, plus flour or cornmeal for
   dusting cookie sheet or pizza peel
6 ounces roasted red bell pepper
   (2 peppers), homemade or from a
   jar, drained

1 can (14 ounces) diced tomatoes,
   drained very well
A couple pinches dried oregano
1/4 pound very thinly sliced
   pepperoni
3/4 pound fresh mozzarella, thinly
   sliced

The oven and pizza stone (see Note) should be preheating at 500°F, as mentioned on page 179.

Lightly flour a clean work surface. Pizza makers should flour their hands and place a ball of dough that has rested for a full hour in the middle of the work space. How you divide toppings depends on the size of the pies you are making. Divide toppings before you start into as many piles as you need.

Roll and flatten and stretch each ball of dough into a disk with a little rim around the edge. Helpers should transfer the pies to a cookie sheet or pizza peel (wooden paddle) dusted with a little more flour or cornmeal. Top each pizza with a few red pepper strips, a sprinkle of tomato bits, a pinch of oregano, a few slices of pepperoni, and a few disks of mozzarella. Go easy! Too many toppings make soggy pizza pie—YUCK! A lightly dressed pie will be super YUMMY! Helpers should drizzle each pie with a touch of olive oil just before it goes in the oven. Slide pizza

"Measuring for me is like a cage," says Italian chef and mom Marcella Hazan. Do not make kids measure with instuments unless an exception is noted in the recipe. These recipes are written with friendly guidelines and equivalents that will teach kids that cooking can be fun and easy.

Measuring by eye and touch—a pinch of this, a dash of that—will build confidence and sharpen instincts, as well as inspire creativity in the kitchen as little kids grow into big kids into the oven and onto a preheated pizza stone. Cook pies 10 to 15 minutes, until golden brown and crispy. Remove from pizza stone using a cookie sheet or peel.

Note: If you do not have a pizza stone, place a cookie sheet dusted with cornmeal on the center rack of oven and preheat for only 15 minutes.

Four Cheeses Pizzas

Makes four 6-inch or two 8-inch pies or one large pie.

1 recipe It's Dough Easy
1 cup prepared pizza sauce or
   tomato sauce
4 ounces each grated provolone,
   mozzarella, and Asiago

1/4 cup grated Parmigiano Reggiano
   cheese
A pinch per pie of chopped fresh or
   dried oregano

Follow method described in Pepper-Pepperoni Pizza for forming the dough. Top each pizza with a very thin layer of sauce, spreading the sauce from the center out to the edges. Sprinkle evenly with cheeses and a pinch of oregano. Cook 8 to 10 minutes, or until cheese is golden and bubbling.

VARIATIONS

Ham and Cheese Pizzas

Makes four 6-inch or two 8-inch pies or one large pie.

1 recipe It's Dough-Easy
1 cup prepared pizza sauce or
   tomato sauce
2 cups, total, shredded Italian
   cheeses (provolone, Asiago,
   mozzarella)

1/4 pound prosciutto di Parma,
   chopped
A pinch fresh or dried oregano
   per pie

Helpers should do the chopping. Follow preceding method for preparation, sprinkling with cheese, prosciutto, and oregano before pie goes in oven.

Veggie Pizzas

Makes four 6-inch or two 8-inch pies or one large pie.

1 recipe It's Dough-Easy

1 cup prepared pizza or tomato sauce

2 cups shredded Italian cheeses (asiago, provolone, mozzarella)

1/2 red bell pepper, seeded and chopped

1/2 green bell pepper, seeded and chopped

A handful oil-cured pitted black olives

1 cup defrosted, drained, chopped broccoli

A pinch fresh or dry thyme for each pie

Helpers should do the chopping for kids under 12. Follow preceding method of preparation. Do not put too many veggies on 1 pie or bunch them up on any area of a pie or your pizzas will be soggy and yucky.

Grown-ups, listen up!

Keep your cool! Never grab a kid's arm or speak harshly to a kid cook unless he or she is in real danger of burn or injury. Let them make mistakes. You can always scoop out too much of something, add a little more of something else, or start from scratch if necessary. All of these options are better solutions than making kids feel as self-conscious as so many adults are about cooking. Food should be fun. Cooking is a celebration of all the good things we have to be thankful for in life, including little kids.

Eggcellent Sandwiches

Makes 6 sandwiches.

9 large eggs
1 tablespoon butter, diced into bits
by Helper, plus 1 tablespoon for
cooking

¹/₃ pound smoked ham (from the
deli counter, in thick slices), diced
into small bits
6 sandwich-size English muffins
6 slices Muenster cheese (from deli)

Kids take turns cracking eggs into bowl and whisking them together with butter bits.

Helpers should dice ham for kids under 10 or supervise dicing, allowing kids to use serrated paring knives—anyone chopping anything needs to always keep their eyes on the board and their fingertips curled under. Place ham bits in a small dish near the stove.

Kids toast English muffins in toaster and place 6 halves on a cookie sheet; pile the tops on a plate.

Helpers heat a nonstick skillet over medium heat. Melt the tablespoon of butter in pan and distribute by tilting pan. Add ham and cook for 2 minutes. Add eggs to pan and allow kids to stir gently with a wooden spoon for 4 to 5 minutes, or until eggs are scrambled and beginning to firm up. Helpers distribute the eggs onto the 6 muffin bottoms on a cookie sheet. Kids top each egg-piled muffin with 1 slice of Muenster cheese. Helpers place cookie sheet under preheated broiler to just melt the cheese. Remove from oven. Top with muffin caps and serve warm.

Miss Jessica's Tar Pit Pterodactyl Wings

Makes up to 30 pieces.

1 cup low-sodium soy sauce
2 tablespoons sesame oil
$^1/_2$ cup apple juice
2 tablespoons apple cider vinegar

$^1/_4$ teaspoon (a couple pinches)
  ground ginger
$^1/_2$ cup brown sugar
3 pounds chicken drumsticks
  (drummers)

Preheat oven to 375°F.

Kids mix all the ingredients except the chicken in a pot. Helpers place the pot over medium-low heat.

Kids stir the sauce until sugar dissolves.

Kids arrange the drummers in a big shallow roasting pan in a single layer. Helpers pour the sauce evenly over the drummers. Helpers place the drummers in the oven for 60 to 75 minutes, turning the drummers once after 35 minutes, giving them a good basting at the same time. Remove drummers to a platter and let cool before little fingers grab them.

Taco Pockets II

For 6 burger wraps, to yield 12 pockets.

Even better than the original recipe—and kids love them even more!

1¹/2 pounds lean ground beef
1 ounce (a lunch-box-size bagful)
    crushed tortilla chips or nacho
    cheese tortilla chips
2 tablespoons (a grown-up palmful)
    dark chili powder
1 tablespoon ground cumin (half a
    grown-up palmful)
4 drops cayenne pepper sauce
2 tablespoons (a splash) water
A couple pinches coarse salt

6 flour tortilla wraps, plain or cheese
    flavored
One 6-ounce jar mild taco sauce
1 heart romaine, shredded
3 plum tomatoes, seeded and diced
    by Helpers
1 sack (10 ounces) shredded Mexican
    cheeses (You can buy a combo
    pack of Asedero, Monterey Jack,
    cheddar, and queso fresco.)

Set the oven on Warm.

Kids, dump the meat into a big bowl and roll up your sleeves! Crush the tortilla chips over the bowl of meat, with your hands, into tiny bits. Helpers can add the chili powder, cumin, cayenne sauce, water, and salt. Now, everyone, get your hands in there and mix the spices in well. Make 6 hamburger-shaped patties and place them on a plate. If you have trouble making a burger shape, roll a handful of meat into a ball, place it on a plate, and flatten it—SQUISH!

Helpers heat a nonstick griddle or skillet over medium-high heat and cook burgers, 3 at a time, for 5 minutes on each side—kids can help with the flips.

Pile the burgers on a plate in the warm oven while you cook the tortillas.

Wipe out the skillet and return to heat. Helpers should warm and blister the tortillas for 30 seconds on each side, then pile them up on a work surface for the kids. Helpers can line up toppings, tortillas, and burgers in a row.

To assemble, kids paint the center of each tortilla with taco sauce by using a pastry brush. Next, pile up a little lettuce and tomato in the center of your tortilla. Now pile some cheese on top and then place a taco burger on top of the cheese and squish it down a bit. Fold the top and bottom edges of the tortilla up and over burger, and twist the entire tortilla a half turn. Flip the last 2 flaps up and turn the entire packet upside down, leaving you with a square-shaped packet. Helpers can be an especially big help with the folding up of the packets. Helpers, cut the packets diagonally from corner to corner and there you have it—2 pockets.

Chicken Tacos

Makes 8 tacos.

There are raisins in this taco filling. Yes, raisins. Get over it and trust me that it's delicious and kids everywhere love it, so just make it—okay?

1 tablespoon extra-virgin olive oil (once around the pan)

1 1/2 pounds boneless, skinless chicken breasts, cut into small cubes

1 small onion, chopped

1 clove garlic, minced

A grown-up handful golden raisins

A handful coarsely chopped Spanish olives stuffed with pimientos

1 cup tomato puree

2 teaspoons chili powder (half a grown-up palmful)

1 teaspoon ground cumin (half as much as the chili powder)

Coarse salt, to taste

8 jumbo corn taco shells

TOPPINGS

Shredded cheeses (smoked cheddar, Monterey Jack, or Pepper Jack)

Avocado dices

Tomato dices

Chopped green onions

Shredded lettuce

Helpers should do the chopping for kids under 12. If the kids must chop, let them do it one at a time, using a small paring knife. Fingers must always be kept tucked in, either on the handle of the knife or curled around and under while holding whatever you are chopping.

Helpers heat the oil in a skillet over medium-high heat. Kids can stir if they use a long wooden spoon and keep their faces away from the pan. Brown the diced chicken bits until lightly golden. Add onion and garlic and cook another couple of minutes to soften onion. Dump in raisins, olives, tomato puree, and seasonings. Sprinkle in a couple of pinches of coarse salt (and throw 1 pinch over your left shoulder, for luck). Bring your taco filling to a bubble, then turn the heat down to low and simmer until ready to serve. Warm taco shells in oven according to package directions. Scoop filling into shells and top them at the table. Feeds up to 6 with a chunked vegetable or green salad.

Meatball Patty Melts

Makes 6 melts

1 pound meat loaf mix (ground beef, pork, and veal) or ground beef only
1 egg
1/2 cup (a couple grown-up handfuls) Italian bread crumbs
1/4 cup (a handful) grated Parmigiano or Romano cheese

A grown-up palmful chopped fresh flatleaf parsley
2 cloves garlic, minced by Helpers
1 small onion, finely chopped by Helpers
1 cup pizza or tomato sauce
6 slices sharp provolone cheese
6 sesame-seeded hard rolls

Kids, wash your hands and roll up your sleeves! In a BIG bowl, mix meat, egg, bread crumbs, cheese, parsley, garlic, and onion. Take turns with the mixing—this is the really fun part!

Next, kids can form meat mixture into 6 hamburger-shaped patties. If you have trouble making a pattie, roll some meat up into a big ball. Put the ball on a plate or cutting board and squish it flat.

Helpers can heat a griddle or nonstick skillet lightly coated with a touch of olive oil or cooking spray over medium-high heat. Cook 3 patties at a time for 4 or 5 minutes on each side. Kids can do the flipping with a long-handled spatula. Top patties with a couple of spoonfuls of pizza or tomato sauce and 1 slice of cheese. Reduce heat to low. Cover pot with lid or cover skillet with a loose aluminum foil tent and let stand 3 to 5 minutes to melt cheese and warm sauce.

Split rolls and fill with meatball pattie melts. Serve with a mixed green salad or a chunked vegetable salad.

D Is for Dumplings

Makes 20 dumplings.

1/2 pound ground pork (available at custom butcher counter)

1 can (8 ounces) water chestnuts, drained well and chopped in a food processor by Helpers

2 green onions, chopped by Helpers

2 tablespoons soy sauce (2 splashes)

2 shakes garlic powder (about 1/4 teaspoon)

4 shakes ground ginger (about 1/2 teaspoon)

A pinch or two cayenne pepper (about 1/8 teaspoon)

A couple pinches coarse salt (and 1 to throw over your shoulder for luck)

1/2 orange, outer skin grated by Helpers, juice squeezed into a small dish by kids

1 egg white, separated by Helpers and lightly beaten

20 wonton wrappers (available in the produce section of the market)

1 cup prepared plum sauce for dipping (available on Asian foods aisle) or cut open all the duck sauce packets you horde in the kitchen drawer each time you get take-out Chinese food

Kids, wash up, and roll up those sleeves! Dump pork, water chestnuts, green onions, soy sauce, garlic powder, spices, salt, grated orange peel, the orange juice, and egg white into a BIG bowl.

Mush everything all together really well. Wash up again and dry off your hands.

Kids take a small pile of wonton wraps stacked on a plate and a teaspoon. Place the bowl in the middle of the counter so everyone can reach in. Scoop out a heaping teaspoon of the filling and place it in the center of a wonton wrapper. Pull up all the sides and pinch the ends together so that the dumpling looks like a small purse or pouch. Place the finished dumplings on a plate and keep making them till the pile of wontons and the filling are all used up.

Helpers need to place a bamboo steamer over a pot of simmering water, or place a metal colander over a larger pot filled with some water for steam—water must not touch the bottom of the steamer or colander.

Helpers can steam the dumplings in a single layer if they have a bamboo steamer. Cook only half a batch at a time in a colander, to prevent clumping. Fit the cover on your bamboo steamer tightly or seal the top of the colander completely with aluminum foil. Steam dumplings over a low simmer for 20 minutes.

> **Whenever you use cayenne pepper, wash your hands with soap right away and NEVER touch your eyes before you do or WOW will it hurt and sting and burn and make you cry, a lot.**

Place on the edges of a serving plate with a small dish of plum or duck sauce in the center of the plate.

D is for delicious!

Chicken Stick-ens

Makes 18 to 20 chicken skewers.

8-inch bamboo skewers(18 to 20)
2 packages chicken tenders, 1 to 1¹/3
pounds total (18 to 20 pieces)
3 to 4 tablespoons (a couple good
scoops) hoisin sauce (found on
Asian foods aisle)
3 tablespoons low-sodium soy sauce
(3 splashes)

2 tablespoons honey (a big drizzle
from the honey bear)
2 tablespoons sesame oil (twice
around the bowl)
A couple shakes ground ginger (about
¹/2 teaspoon
A meat mallet
Waxed paper

Soak the skewers in a shallow dish of water.

Cover a work surface with a sheet of waxed paper and place the chicken tenders in a single layer across the surface. Top with a second sheet of waxed paper. Here comes the fun part: Kids can take turns whacking the chicken with a meat mallet to flatten the strips out. (Those of you in Little League or Tee-ball, watch it! Don't whack the chicken so hard that it dents the counter, okay?)

Now, pull back the top layer of waxed paper and thread the skewers one at a time, very carefully—skewers hurt when you poke them into your fingers, trust me. Poke the skewers in and out of the chicken meat till you get to the end of the tender. Helpers, keep your eyes peeled and your hands free to shadow small kids while they perform this step.

Wash up before you do another thing and do not touch anything or anyone until you do. Thank you.

Mix hoisin sauce, soy sauce, honey, sesame oil, and ginger in a small bowl.

Place the chicken sticks in a baking dish or shallow platter and pour the sauce over them. Turn the skewers all around to coat the chicken evenly in the sauce.

Wash up again.

Helpers, heat a big skillet or non-stick griddle pan over high heat. Using tongs to turn, cook skewers 3 minutes on each side in a single layer, half a batch at a time. If the pan smokes a lot, reduce heat a little.

Allow the chicken sticks to cool to room temperature before little hands pick them up.

Helpers and kids should always wash hands, utensils, and work surfaces after handling raw meats. This is very important. Heat, while cooking, can kill any bad germs growing on the meat, but, using the same utensils or using dirty hands to handle or chop things that will not be cooked will transfer the bad germs from the meat to the other foods.

Kids' No-Pain Lo Mein

For 6 side-dish portions.

Helpers, put a big pot of water on the stove to boil for pasta. Cook ½ **pound spaghetti** until al dente, 8 minutes or so. Drain noodles well.

Kids, dump the following into a blender:

½ cup creamy peanut butter (a couple heaping scoops)

3 tablespoons soy sauce (3 good splashes)

1 tablespoon sesame oil (found on Asian foods aisle)

2 pinches cayenne pepper (about ¼ teaspoon)

2 shakes garlic powder (about ¼ teaspoon)

3 shakes ground ginger (about ½ teaspoon)

A drizzle honey

⅓ cup warm water

Pulse the blender until the sauce has an even and smooth consistency.

Toss the noodles with sauce in a big bowl and mix in:

2 green onions, thinly sliced by Helpers

1 carrot, grated by Helpers

½ red bell pepper, seeded and chopped by Helpers

YUM! Place a pile of noodles on a plate with some of your own homemade dumplings or your chicken on a stick.

Sack-o-Fish

Makes 6 sacks.

Pastry brushes
6 brown or white paper lunch sacks
A dish holding a few ounces
   vegetable oil
4 tablespoons butter
3 tablespoons all-purpose flour (a
   handful)
1 cup chicken broth
A pinch Old Bay seasoning or
   poultry seasoning

Juice of 1/2 lemon, plus 6 thin slices
   of lemon from the other half,
   sliced by Helpers
A sprinkle freshly ground pepper
Six 4-ounce chunks of cod or
   haddock, rinsed and patted dry
   with paper towels, *lightly sprinkled
   with salt*
12 sea scallops, drained and
   patted dry

Preheat oven to 350°F with racks on second-up-from-bottom and top shelves.

Kids, take pastry brushes in hand and paint the paper sacks, front and back, with a thin coating of vegetable oil. Open the sacks and line them up on their sides on a cookie sheet, 3 or 4 to a pan.

Helpers, heat a small skillet or shallow saucepan over medium heat. Kids, add butter to the pan and when it melts, sprinkle in flour while Helper gently whisks it into the butter. This is called a "roux" (pronounced like Tigger and Roo). *Roux* is a French word for this funny paste of flour and butter that will thicken a sauce. The starch in the flour will expand and cook in the sauce and make a thin liquid turn thick. Cook your roux for 3 or 4 minutes, then slowly add the chicken broth, seasoning, lemon juice, and a little pepper while the Helper keeps stirring. Bring the sauce to a bubble and then turn the heat down a little and let the sauce reduce (get smaller) until it has thickened and will coat and stick to a spoon—about 10 minutes is all it should take.

Take the sauce off the stove and pour it into a bowl.

Now, everyone take a piece of fish and place a thin slice of lemon on top. Place the fish in the center of your bag. Place two scallops in the bag next to the fish. One at a time, pass the bowl of sauce around and take a couple of spoonfuls of sauce and carefully pour them over the fish in the center of the bag.

Next, carefully fold the edges of your bag under. Tuck them under tightly. Make sure your bag is sealed well or your sauce will all run out and away like the last little piggy.

Helpers, place the bags on 2 racks in the oven and cook for 15 minutes.

Remove the sacks and carefully transfer each one to a plate. Helpers, cut the tops of bags from one end to the other with scissors, watching that no little fingers get in the way of escaping steam. Open the bags enough to expose the pretty garnished fish and scallops. Eat with lots of warm rolls to soak up the juice. Mmmmmmmmmm—good.

Meat-Bit-Bites

Makes 24.

1¹/2 pounds boneless top sirloin
   steak, trimmed of all fat and
   connective tissue
¹/4 cup Worcestershire
3 tablespoons butter, melted
Montreal Steak Seasoning (by
   Mc Cormick)

2 cloves of garlic
1 tablespoon extra-virgin olive oil
2 or 3 tablespoons of water

Toothpicks or bamboo skewers, for
   dipping

Helpers, prepare meat: chop meat into bite-size chunks, about 24 pieces.

Let it stand at room temperature while sauce is prepared. (Meat should never be cooked directly from cold storage to hot pan. It toughens from the shock.)

Kids, arrange bits on a cookie sheet.

Kids, combine Worcestershire and melted butter in a small dish.

Kids, take pastry brushes (kitchen paintbrushes) and brush the meat bits with a little of the special sauce in the dish.

Sprinkle the bits with Montreal Steak Seasoning.

Kids, wash up.

Kids, whack garlic with a meat mallet to take it out of its skin.

Helpers, heat olive oil, once around the pan, in a big nonstick skillet over high heat.

Add garlic and meat bits and sear for 2 minutes on each side. Add a splash of water to deglaze the pan and scrape up any good gunk. Remove pan from heat and let stand 5 minutes.

Transfer bits to a platter and serve as is with toothpicks for eating or place alongside chili fondue (recipe follows) and dip with long bamboo skewers or fondue forks, along with corn chips or bread chunks.

Fun-to-Do Fon-Dude

Makes enough dip for 24 to 36 pieces or a lot of chips.

A cheezy-chili dip for bread, chips, or Meat-Bit-Bites (preceding recipe).

One 8-ounce brick cream cheese OR 1 jar (16 ounces) prepared low-fat con queso sauce (available on the snack foods aisle)

1 can (16 ounces) Hormel chili with no beans

1 bag corn tortilla chips OR chunks of crusty bread OR 1 recipe Meat-Bit-Bites

A fondue pot and forks OR preheated Pyrex bowl, warmed in oven handled by Helpers

Bamboo party skewers for dipping

Kids, dump the cream cheese or cheese sauce and chili into a small saucepan and take turns stirring over low heat until the cream cheese melts and/or dip comes to a bubble.

Helpers, transfer the sauce into a fondue pot or a warm Pyrex bowl and start dipping! If you use bread, place chunks on the tip of a fondue fork. (Chips you can dip with no assistance.) If you are using Meat-Bit-Bites, prepare the bites first, then the dip.

Meatza Pizza Balls

1 pound 93% lean ground beef
1/4 pound pepperoni, chopped by
    Helpers into small bits
1 egg
1/2 cup Italian bread crumbs
    (a couple of grown-up handfuls)
1/4 cup grated Parmigiano or Romano
    cheese (a grown-up palmful)

2 shakes fresh or dried oregano
    (about 1/4 teaspoon)
3 shakes garlic powder (about 1/2
    teaspoon)
A couple pinches coarse salt (plus one
    to throw over your shoulder for luck)
1 can (14 ounces) prepared pizza
    sauce or tomato sauce
Toothpicks, for dipping

Preheat oven to 425°F.

Kids, wash up, and roll up sleeves. Combine meat, pepperoni, egg, bread crumbs, cheese, oregano, garlic poweder, and salt in a big bowl. Squish everything up with your hands, really mixing all the spices and special ingredients into the meat.

Wash up. Thank you.

Helpers, place a nonstick cookie sheet or a baking sheet coated with cooking spray or brushed with olive oil in the center of the work space. Have a bowl of warm water ready for dampening small hands before they roll meatballs.

Kids, dip your hands into the bowl of warm water. Now, grab a small lump of meat and roll it between the palms of your hands to make a ball, then drop it onto the cookie sheet. Helpers, guide little hands and keep an eye out to make sure the balls are fairly consistent in size, about 1 inch in diameter, so that the cooking time will be the same for all of the meatballs.

When all the balls are rolled, wash up again.

Helpers, place the cookie sheet on the middle rack of the oven and bake for 10 to 12 minutes or until balls are evenly browned. Loosen balls with a spatula about midway through baking if you are not using a nonstick cookie sheet. Break 1 ball open to test and make sure there is no pink left in the meat before removing from oven.

While balls are in oven, warm pizza or tomato sauce on stovetop. Transfer to a small bowl and place in the middle of a serving platter. Scatter balls all around the dip and place a small glass filled with toothpicks alongside for dipping.

A little music adds to any party and relaxes every cook. Mix it up! Play a little samba and swing along with kids' favorites. Kids can bring their own chart-topping tapes or disks to the gathering and take turns sharing their tastes. (After-dinner dancing is also highly recommended.)

Stuffed Stalks

Makes 18 3-inch-long stuffed celery pieces.

6 stalks celery, cut in 3-inch pieces
One 8-ounce brick cream cheese,
  softened to room temperature
3 tablespoons (a couple scoops from
  the jar) sliced green olives with
  pimiento

2 sprinkles paprika
Fresh flat-leaf parsley, for garnish,
  finely chopped by Helpers

Helpers, blanch celery in boiling water for 20 seconds to kill any bacteria in stalks. Drain and run under cold water until celery has cooled entirely. Dry celery with paper towels before stuffing.

Kids, mix cream cheese, olives, and the couple of sprinkles paprika in a small bowl, taking turns stirring until olives are evenly distributed in the cream cheese. Kids, take turns mounding stalks of celery with cream cheese mixture using a spoon and a small butter knife. Sprinkle the stuffed stalks with chopped parsley and chill until ready to serve.

Veggie Dip with Zip

Recipe will be enough to dip 3 to 4 dozen vegetable pieces.

One 4-ounce brick cream cheese,
  softened to room temperature

1 small jar (6 ounces) mild taco sauce
2 green onions, thinly sliced by
  Helpers

Kids, mix these ingredients in a small bowl until smooth. Place dip in a pretty dish to serve, surrounded by your favorite veggie sticks, broccoli and cauliflower florets, fresh green beans, and cherry tomatoes.

Sticks can be made for kids by Helpers out of carrot, celery, European seedless cucumber, zucchini, yellow squash, red, yellow, and green bell peppers—whatever favorites are in season.

Helpers should blanch the veggies by dipping in boiling water for 20 to 30 seconds, then draining and cold-shocking them with running water until they are cool. Pat dry before arranging on platter for dipping.

Deviled Ham Dip

Recipe will dip up to 30 vegetable sticks or cover 24 crackers or bread

1 can (5 ounces) deviled ham
One 4-ounce brick softened cream
    cheese

1 rounded teaspoon Dijon mustard
Paprika and chopped fresh parsley,
    for garnish, chopped by Helpers
    for kids under 12

For dipping or spreading, mix and match your favorites:
- Celery sticks, blanched, cold-shocked, and dried
- Carrot sticks, blanched, cold-shocked, and dried
- Crackers: saltines, Ritz, Triscuits—whatever you like
- Breads: rye, pumpernickel, white, wheat—toasted
      and cut into quarters for dipping or spreading

Mix ham, cream cheese, and and mustard in a small bowl. Scrape into a serving dish for dipping. The dip is thick, so only carrot and celery will be strong enough for veggie dipping. Crackers or toast will need a butter knife or party spreader for serving.

Creamsicle Fruit Dip

Recipe will dip up to 40 pieces of fruit.

1 box vanilla instant pudding mix
1 1/4 cups milk

1 can (6 ounces) orange juice
    concentrate, thawed

Kids, stir milk and pudding mix together in a big bowl. When pudding mix has dissolved, add orange juice concentrate and stir until the dip is evenly orange in color. Transfer dip to a dip dish and chill in fridge until ready to eat.

Serve with chunks of fresh pineapple, melon, and berries, available already cleaned and chopped in the produce section of market.

The Ultimate Peanut Butter Kiss Cookies

Makes 60 cookies.

My mom found this recipe in a magazine and made them even better by putting a chocolate kiss on top—her cookies are really cool. I have to give you one serious warning though: Peanut butter cups will never taste as good as they used to once you eat these cookies.

1 cup chunky peanut butter	1 teaspoon baking soda (This one
1 cup sugar	you have to really measure.)
1 large egg	60 chocolate kisses (2 bags)

Kids, unwrap all the chocolate kisses and pile them up on a plate. Try not to sneak'n-eat too many or you won't have enough for the cookies.

Preheat oven to 350°F and lightly grease 2 cookie sheets with cooking spray or softened butter.

Kids, beat peanut butter and sugar in a big bowl on medium speed until the sugar is all mixed into the peanut butter. Beat an egg and baking soda in a smaller bowl and pour into peanut butter mixture. Beat again on medium speed until the egg is all combined into the peanut butter.

Kids, scoop out dough a teaspoonful at a time and roll it into a small ball. Place the balls at least 1 inch apart on cookie sheet and squish a kiss down on top of each ball, nesting it into the dough.

Place no more than 30 cookies on each cookie sheet. Bake in hot oven for 10 minutes. Remove and transfer to a cooling rack with a metal spatula, being careful not to stick your fingers in the kisses—the chocolate will be too soft. Let cookies cool completely before gobbling.

Kids Cooking Party Pointers and Table Tips

Call up your local newspaper and ask them if you can come by and pick up the ends of their paper rolls. Most newspapers will be only to glad to give you hundreds of feet of scrap-paper-on-a-roll. Cover any dining table, big coffee table, or picnic table with long sheets torn from the paper roll and tape edges down to secure. Let kids decorate their table by drawing on the paper table cover with crayons or washable markers. For an easy seating idea, surround your coffee table with big pillows.

The Filiacis' Famous Banana-Nut Chocolate-Chip Bread

Makes 1 loaf.

Brought to us by three kids who love to cook—Alex, Renata, and Sabia Rose.

3/4 cup sugar
1/4 cup butter
2 large eggs
2 large or 3 small ripe bananas, mashed
2 cups all-purpose unbleached flour

2 teaspoons baking powder
1/2 teaspoon salt
1/4 teaspoon baking soda
1 cup semisweet chocolate chips
1 cup chopped walnuts

Preheat oven 350°F. Lightly grease a 9 by 5 by 3-inch loaf pan. Cream sugar, butter, and eggs together until fluffy. Fold in mashed bananas with a spoon. Sift dry ingredients into a large mixing bowl. Add banana mixture, chocolate chips, and walnuts to the dry ingredients and stir until smooth. Pour batter into the loaf pan and bake 55 minutes, or until toothpick inserted in cake comes out clean. Let cool before removing from pan.

For a fun and edible party craft, buy different shapes and sizes of bulk candies at the market. Pick up a couple of small tubes of prepared icing so little hands can draw with them. Cut thin licorice whips into strips. Place all the toppings on a tray and let kids make up faces and creatures on the tops of frosted cupcakes. Halloween cupcakes can be turned into spiders and goblins. Christmas cupcakes can look like ornaments. Birthday cupcakes can be turned into favorite animals. Spice cake mix, made to low-fat directions on the box by adding applesauce, makes a nice cupcake that appeals to everyone. This will help you avoid fights over the last chocolate or the last vanilla cupcake. Cream cheese frosting, homemade or storebought, makes a good canvas for the toppings.

Oh My Gosh, That's Good Ganache!

Dips up to 18 pieces of fresh or dried fruit.

Ganache is French for a chocolate coating that is often used to cover cakes or fruits. It is YUMMY dipped onto big, sweet strawberries or dried fruits like apricots and peaches.

8 ounces semisweet chocolate morsels

1/4 cup heavy (whipping) cream
2 drops vanilla extract

Melt morsels and cream over lowest heat and stir until smooth, about 5 minutes. Stir in vanilla. Dip berries or dried fruits in the chocolate and set them on a wax paper–lined plate or pan. Chill to set chocolate, then serve.

Mocktails

Sunrise Fizz

Cranberry juice
Orange juice

Splash ginger ale
Orange slice, for garnish

Fill a glass 3/4 of the way up with equal parts cranberry juice and orange juice. Fill glass to the top with ginger ale. Garnish with a slice of orange.

Bahama Mama Mocktail

Grenadine
Pineapple juice
Lemon-lime soda or seltzer

Slice of citrus or pineapple wedge, for garnish

Pour a splash of grenadine in your glass. Fill the glass halfway with pineapple juice. Fill the glass up to the top with lemon-lime soda or seltzer and garnish with sliced citrus or pineapple wedge.

Grape Ape Fizz

Grenadine
Grape juice

Lime seltzer
Fruit slice or cherry, for garnish

Pour a splash of grenadine in the bottom of your glass. Fill the glass halfway with grape juice. Fill up to the top of the glass with lime seltzer and garnish with fruit slice or a cherry.

Lemon Freeze

Lemonade concentrate
Vanilla ice milk
Lime seltzer or lemon-lime soda

1 scoop sherbet or paper umbrella, for garnish

Pour 2 ounces ($1/3$ can) of defrosted lemonade concentrate in a blender. Add 2 scoops ice milk and a splash of soda or seltzer and blend until smooth. Pour into a tall glass or party cup and garnish with a melon ball scoop of sherbet or a paper umbrella.

Creamsicle Freeze Fizz

Light cream or half-and-half
Orange sherbet
7-UP or other lemon-lime soda

Scoop lime sherbet or whipped cream and paper umbrella, for garnish

Pour 2 ounces (2 splashes or 2 tablespoons) of cream or half-and-half into a blender. Add 2 scoops of orange sherbet and a splash of 7-UP or soda. Blend until smooth and top with a melon ball scoop of lime sherbet or a little whipped cream and a paper umbrella.

Just Desserts

Quick Simple Treats

Sweets for the Baking Impaired

Many cooks cannot bake. I am one of them.

Cooks feel their way through recipes—a pinch of this, a pinch of that. Cooking is a messy, ever-changing improvisation until the food hits the plate. Baking is a delicate pursuit, more akin to a science than an art. Baking demands exact measures, attention to detail, and an adherence to proven methods of doing things. It is a choreographed ballet—a perfect marriage of self-expression and self-discipline, joy and patience. I was a crummy ballet student. I kept breaking out into my own awkward twitches and convulsions. I complained that the teacher didn't know how to dance.

I appreciate the controlled effort, the ability to be creative within a set of constraints, that bakers have. Their commitment brings remarkable things to the world. My scales are forever tipped in one direction. I have not the patience to work for the balance. Cooks with patience become chefs—schooled to create desserts to match the beauty of their meals. I am not a chef. I am just a cook who feels tiny when I look at a beautifully painted Christmas cookie or a seven-layer cake, at once awestruck and completely aware of how little I know.

For me, dessert comes from the bakery. As dinosaurs can be seen only in museums, pretty and sweet things were viewed only outside my kitchen. Until now.

"Just Desserts" is a collection (albeit it a very small one) of recipes for those who, like me, feel inadequate once the dinner plates are cleared. In facing my fears about this dreaded course, I was forced to recall old favorites and create new solutions. Sweets will no longer taunt me—not even the evil, perfectly decorated gingerbread men that visit me in my nightmares every December. Non-bakers unite and, bakers, please skip this section of the book. You won't be impressed and you will only think of ways to improve on it. Leave us non-bakers with a little dignity.

Fabulous, Foolproof Fudges

Deep Chocolate Fudge with Walnuts and Currants

Makes a 2 1/2- to 3-pound ring.

Butter, softened, to grease cake pan
12 ounces semisweet chocolate chips
8 ounces butterscotch chips, about
$3/4$ of an 11-ounce bag (Snack on the rest.)
1 can (14 ounces) sweetened condensed milk

1 can (8 ounces) walnut halves
$1/2$ teaspoon vanilla extract (a couple drops)
A handful currants (about $1/4$ cup, packed)

Grease the inside of an 8-inch round cake pan with a little softened butter and set aside. In a heavy-bottomed pot, melt chocolate and butterscotch chips together with sweetened condensed milk over low heat. Save sweetened condensed milk can and set aside. Stir constantly until the mixture is smooth. Remove from heat immediately. Stir in nuts, vanilla, and currants. Cover milk can with plastic wrap and place in the center of the cake pan. Scoop fudge out of pot and into cake pan, keeping the milk can centered in the pan. Do not smooth the top down—the bumpy, rounded peaks will enhance the appearance of the chocolate wreath that is taking shape. Cool the fudge wreath to room temperature, or chill. Remove the can by twisting it free. Turn pan upside down and carefully twist pan free from wreath. Place wreath textured side up on a plate and decorate with holiday ribbons, floral sprigs, or ornaments. Serve fudge in small slivers—it is very rich.

VARIATION:

For Fancy Fudge-Filled Packages: Scoop warm fudge into a greased 9 by 9-inch square pan. Cool and cut into 1- to $1 1/2$-inch-square pieces. Cut 4-inch lengths of 3-inch-wide holiday ribbon with wire trim (available at craft stores). Place fudge in center of ribbon. Wrap sides of ribbon up and over fudge cube. Twist each end of ribbon. Fill paper holiday cones, sleighs, or small baskets with tiny fudge-filled packages for fast and easy gift giving. One recipe of any fudge makes up to 81 wrapped pieces.

White Chocolate Fudge with Pistachios and Cranberries

20 ounces white chocolate chips
  (1 3/4 packages)
1 can (14 ounces) sweetened
  condensed milk

1/2 teaspoon vanilla extract
  (a couple drops)
8 ounces shelled natural pistachios
A handful dried cranberries (available in produce sections)

Follow method described in Deep Chocolate Fudge with Walnuts and Currants recipe, page 205.

Peppermint Fudge

8 ounces hard peppermint candies
  (white candies with green and red
  stripes)
20 ounces white chocolate chips
  (1 1/2 packages)

1 can (14 ounces) sweetened
  condensed milk
1/2 teaspoon vanilla extract
  (a couple drops)

Crush peppermint candies by placing them in a Baggie and beating with a blunt object. Set aside. Follow method described in Deep Chocolate Fudge with Walnuts and Fudge, page 205. Stir in candy when fudge mixture has been removed from heat.

Ice Cream Dreams
Four No-Brainer Desserts from the Freezer

Café au Lait

Makes 8 servings.

¹/₂ pint heavy (whipping) cream
1 to 2 tablespoons sugar
1 drop vanilla extract

2 pints coffee ice cream
4 jiggers coffee liqueur
3 tablespoons cinnamon sugar

Beat cream with sugar and a drop of vanilla until it just forms peaks. Scoop ice cream into serving dishes. Top each scoop with half a jigger of coffee liqueur and a dollop of whipped cream. Sprinkle with a little cinnamon sugar and serve.

Mexican Sundaes

Serves 8.

8 ounces honey (in a honey bear squeeze bottle)
2 pints vanilla bean ice cream

4 ounces salted Spanish peanuts (the tiny peanuts with skins)

Drizzle a little honey in the bottom of each ice cream dish. Place a scoop of vanilla bean ice cream on top. Drizzle scoops with a little more honey, just enough to glaze the scoops. Sprinkle sundaes with salted Spanish peanuts and serve.

Emmanuel's Melon Bowls

Serves 8.

4 small, ripe cantaloupes
2 pints vanilla ice cream

Halve each melon across the center and scoop out seeds. Fill each melon bowl with scoops of vanilla ice cream and serve.

Nuts and Berries

Serves 8.

4 jiggers hazelnut liqueur
2¹/₂ to 3 cups mixed berries: black berries, raspberries, sliced strawberries

1 tablespoon sugar
8 ounces hazelnuts, crushed and toasted
2 pints vanilla bean ice cream

Pour liqueur over berries and sprinkle with sugar. Let sit during dinner. After meal, scoop a little of the berry mixture into the bottom of serving dishes. Top with ice cream and cover scoops with more berries. Sprinkle with a little of the crushed nuts.

Simple Showstoppers

Quick Lemon Cottage Cake

Serves 8.

1 angel food cake from bakery
    section of market or 1 packaged
    pound cake

1 jar (10 ounces) lemon curd
2 teaspoons water(a splash)
1 lemon

Cut cake into 8 servings. If you're using pound cake, warm slices for 20 seconds in microwave before serving. Dump lemon curd into a small saucepan and warm over low heat with a splash of water. Spoon warm curd over slices of cake to glaze. Zest the lemon with a hand grater and sprinkle zest over glazed cake slices. Serve immediately.

Vicki's Zabaglione

Serves 8.

BERRY TOPPING (OPTIONAL)
2 cups sliced strawberries
1 tablespoon sugar
3 tablespoons marsala

ZABAGLIONE
9 egg yolks
9 tablespoons sugar
9 tablespoons marsala
1 bag ice

Sprinkle berries with sugar and marsala. Set aside.

    Place a stainless steel mixing bowl over a pot of water on medium heat or warm some water in the bottom of a double boiler pan. Do not allow water to touch the bottom of top bowl or pan. Heat water to a low simmer. Beat egg yolks, sugar, and marsala in the top bowl or pan with a whisk until just foamy and mixture begins to thicken. Remove bowl or top pan from heat and place atop a large bowl filled with ice. Continue to beat mixture until it cools and becomes as thick as pudding. Serve zabaglione as is or layer with berries and serve either warm or chilled.

    Thank you, Vicki.

VARIATION:

Zabaglione with Baked Pears

Serves 8.

1 recipe Vicki's Zabaglione

1/2 cup dark or spiced rum

8 ripe pears, Bosc or Anjou, peeled and cored

1 cup dark brown sugar, loosely packed

1/2 stick (4 tablespoons) butter

Prepare zabaglione.

Preheat oven to 375°F. Pour rum into the bottom of a baking dish or casserole. Place pears in dish and sprinkle each with brown sugar and top with half a tablespoon of butter. Cover dish with aluminum foil and cook for 15 minutes. Remove foil and cook another 10 minutes, basting pears frequently. Serve warm pears with a scoop of zabaglione alongside.

Pot de Crème

Makes 6 individual custard cups.

2 cups heavy (whipping) cream

6 ounces semisweet chocolate

2 tablespoons sugar (a scant palmful)

6 egg yolks

1/2 teaspoon vanilla extract

Whipped cream, for topping

Preheat oven to 300°F.

In a heavy saucepan, combine cream, chocolate, and sugar and stir over low heat until chocolate melts and cream is scalding hot. Remove from heat. Beat egg yolks in a bowl. Pour a quarter of the chocolate mixture into the eggs in a very thin stream while stirring. Add egg mixture back to chocolate in a thin stream, stirring constantly. Add vanilla and remove chocolate mixture from stove. Pour into 6 custard cups and cover with aluminum foil. Place in pan filled with 1 inch of water. Place pan in center of oven and bake 20 minutes. Can be served warm or chilled overnight. Top with whipped cream when ready to serve.

Baked Stuffed Apples

Serves 6.

1/2 lemon
6 large Macintosh apples, cored and
   left whole
1/4 stick (2 tablespoons) butter,
   softened
1/2 cup dark brown sugar

3/4 cup chopped walnuts or pecans,
   toasted (about 2 handfuls)
A palmful raisins
A pinch ground nutmeg
2 pinches ground cinnamon
Zest of 1/2 lemon

Preheat oven to 350°F.

Squeeze the juice of 1/2 lemon over apples. Combine softened butter, sugar, nuts, raisins, nutmeg, cinnamon, and lemon zest. Fill apple cavities with this mixture, mounding them a bit at the top. Bake in shallow baking dish with a little water in the bottom of dish for 30 minutes.

Quick Cassata

Serves 8 to 10

Cassata is a Sicilian dessert creation of a sweet, creamed ricotta or semifreddo (half-frozen ice cream) inside thin layers of genoise sponge cake. The cake is often elaborately decorated with almond or hazelnut nougat and fondant.

This recipe for cassata "cake" tastes like a giant cannoli and looks like a million bucks. It is one terrific fake-out.

2 pounds part-skim ricotta
2 cups confectioners' sugar
2 teaspoons ground cinnamon
1/4 cup mini semisweet chocolate chips
1/4 cup chopped candied fruit
1/2 cup chopped pistachios, pine
   nuts, or slivered almonds

2 packages ladyfingers, halved
6 tablespoons marsala (optional)
1 cup seedless raspberry jam
Candied fruits and/or edible flowers
   (optional)

Force the ricotta through a sieve or strainer. Combine with the next 5 ingredients. Line an 8-inch glass bowl to the top with the halved ladyfingers, pressing them gently to conform to the shape of the bowl. Sprinkle with Marsala, if you like. Spread the inside of the lined bowl with a thin layer of raspberry jam. Fill with ricotta mixture. Top the bowl completely with ladyfinger strips. Press down lightly and cover. Refrigerate for at least 4 hours. When ready to serve, place a plate on top of the bowl and turn out the cassata. Sprinkle with powdered sugar and decorate with candied fruits and/or edible flowers.

Index

C

T